just

THE JOB

Working with Children & Young People

*Also published in the **Just the Job!** series:*

just

THE JOB

Working with Children & Young People

Lifetime Careers
WILTSHIRE

Hodder & Stoughton

A MEMBER OF THE HODDER HEADLINE GROUP

Just the Job! draws directly on the CLIPS careers information database developed and maintained by Lifetime Careers Wiltshire and used by almost every careers service in the UK. The database is revised annually using a rigorous update schedule and incorporates material collated through desk/telephone research and information provided by all the professional bodies, institutions and training bodies with responsibility for course accreditation and promotion of each career area.

ISBN 0 340 71139 6
First published 1998

Impression number   10 9 8 7 6 5 4 3 2 1
Year   2002 2001 2000 1999 1998

Printed in Great Britain for Hodder & Stoughton Educational, the educational publishing division of Hodder Headline Plc, 338 Euston Road, London NW1 3BH, by Cox & Wyman Ltd, Reading, Berkshire.

CONTENTS

JUST THE JOB!

The *Just the Job!* series ranges over the entire spectrum of occupations and is intended to generate job ideas and stretch horizons of interest and possibility, allowing you to explore families of jobs for which you might have appropriate ability and aptitude. Each *Just the Job!* book looks in detail at a popular area or type of work, covering:

- ways into work;
- essential qualifications;
- educational and training options;
- working conditions;
- progression routes;
- potential career portfolios.

The information given in *Just the Job!* books is detailed and carefully researched. Obvious bias is excluded to give an even-handed picture of the opportunities available, and course details and entry requirements are positively checked in an annual update cycle by a team of careers information specialists. The text is written in approachable, plain English, with a minimum of technical terms.

In Britain today, there is no longer the expectation of a career for life, but support has increased for life-long learning and the acquisition of skills which will help young and old to make sideways career moves – perhaps several times during a working life – as well as moving into work carrying higher levels of responsibility and reward. *Just the Job!* invites you to select an appropriate direction for your *own* career progression.

Educational and vocational qualifications

A level – Advanced level of the General Certificate of Education

AS level – Advanced Supplementary level of the General Certificate of Education (equivalent to half an A level)

BTEC – Business and Technology Education Council: awards qualifications such as BTEC First, BTEC National Certificate/Diploma, etc

GCSE – General Certificate of Secondary Education

GNVQ/GSVQs – General National Vocational Qualification/ General Scottish Vocational Qualification: awarded at Foundation, Intermediate and Advanced levels by BTEC, City & Guilds, Royal Society of Arts and the Scottish Qualifications Authority (SQA)

HND/C – BTEC Higher National Diploma/Certificate

International Baccalaureate – recognised by all UK universities as equivalent to a minimum of two A levels

NVQ/SVQs – National/Scottish Vocational Qualifications

SCE – Scottish Certificate of Education, at **Standard** Grade (equate directly with GCSEs: grades 1–3 in SCEs at Standard Grade are equivalent to GCSE grades A–C) and **Higher** Grade (equate with the academic level attained after one year of a two-year A level course: three to five Higher Grades are broadly equivalent to two to four A levels at grades A–E)

Vocational work-based credits	NVQ/SVQ level 1	NVQ/SVQ level 2	NVQ/SVQ level 3	NVQ/SVQ level 4
Vocational qualifications: *a mix of theory and practice*	Foundation GNVQ/ GSVQ; BTEC First	Intermediate GNVQ/GSVQ	Advanced GNVQ/GSVQ; BTEC National Diploma/Certificate	BTEC Higher National Diploma/ Certificate
Educational qualifications	GCSE/SCE Standard Grade pass grades	GCSE grades A–C; SCE Standard Grade levels 1–3	Two A levels; four Scottish Highers; Baccalaureate	University degree

INTRODUCTION

For many people, the idea of working with children is very attractive, whether it is with the very young, developing children or with adolescents. Many of the jobs require years of training and high qualifications, but there are also plenty where maturity, a sense of responsibility, a caring attitude and a lively interest in the young can make up for few or no educational qualifications.

Children and young people can be engaging, lively and fun to be with. But ill or disturbed children can be demanding and difficult and require the greatest skill and patience. Don't think for

a moment that working with children will demand any less of you than working with adults. Just ask any infant school teacher after the class has just gone home for Christmas about the joys of working with the reception year!

The range of careers open can be divided into two main types. There are the kinds of job where you train straight away to work with children, such as nursery nursing or infant teaching. Alternatively you can choose the training or education which gives you the opportunity to specialise at a later stage. Examples here would include most medical careers and social work. It might also be possible to start perhaps in artistic, creative work like theatre or music and then work specifically with young people.

In this our modern age you may be vetted quite closely before working with children because, although most people want to work with young people for the very best of reasons, there are those who wish to exploit vulnerable children. Police checks are usually made on people seeking to work in close contact with children and young people.

NURSERY NURSE

Being a nursery nurse means being trained to give a high standard of professional child and family care. The main duties of nursery nurses are to supervise the safety and routine of children in their care. You will normally need a few good GCSEs to be accepted onto a training course.

Nursery nurses work with children, from new-born babies to seven-year-olds, in a variety of settings. They promote the physical, emotional, social and educational development of the children in their care, and provide support, security and a stable environment in which they can thrive. The past few years have seen an increasing emphasis on the pre-school education of children, requiring teaching as well as caring skills from the nursery nurse.

With the number of working mothers continuing to increase, and the availability of nursery places for all four-year-olds, the demand for qualified nursery nurses remains high. Nursery nursing is a career open to both males and females, although relatively few men are employed in nurseries at present. However, the importance of having men, as well as women, to care for children is increasingly realised.

Nursery nurses work in a number of different settings:

- in nurseries, which may be run by local authorities or voluntary organisations or may be privately owned;
- in nursery, infant or special schools, helping the qualified teacher in the planning and the day-to-day running of the

school. The nursery nurse may be responsible for a small group of children doing a wide range of activities;

- in hospitals, working on paediatric wards, organising play activities;
- in private family homes, responsible for all aspects of child-care and development;
- in holiday centres and even on cruise ships – although opportunities on ships are rare.

What it takes

To work as a nursery nurse, you need to:

- like children and enjoy being with them!
- understand child development;
- have endless patience;
- be observant;
- be lively, imaginative and creative;
- have a sense of humour.

QUALIFICATIONS AND TRAINING

NNEB Diploma in Nursery Nursing

This is the main qualification in nursery nursing, awarded by the Council for Awards in Children's Care and Education (CACHE). It is a two-year full-time course, but can also be gained through part-time study. Topics studied include child development, and health and social studies. Most colleges require three GCSEs at grade C for entry to the full diploma course, but other qualifications or a pass in a college entrance test may be sufficient for some colleges, and there is no minimum requirement. English is the most important subject, while subjects like art, music, home economics and child development will provide a useful background.

On some courses it is also possible to be assessed for an NVQ (National Vocational Qualification) in Child Care and Education at level 3.

Mature applicants are welcome and may have previous experience and study taken into consideration, allowing them to qualify in a slightly shorter time.

Getting a place is competitive. Personality is very important, and the better your qualifications, and the more experience you have with children, the greater will be your chance of acceptance.

CACHE Certificate in Child Care and Education (CCE)
This takes a year to complete. Topics include child care, play, health studies and first aid. People who successfully gain this certificate may then be able to take a one-year version of the Diploma course. They may also be able to be assessed for NVQ level 2.

Advanced Diploma in Child Care and Education (ADCE)
The Advanced Diploma is open to people who have already gained childcare qualifications, and is particularly suitable for people who have some years' experience in childcare. The

course builds on your experience and qualifications. It can be studied on a full-time or part-time basis.

GNVQ in Health and Social Care/BTEC National Diploma in Care (Nursery Nursing)

Most further education colleges and some schools offer the GNVQ. The BTEC National Diploma is offered in some FE colleges.

Private nursery colleges

The colleges affiliated to the Association of Nursery Training Colleges normally require three GCSEs at grade C, including English language, for entry to their courses, which are generally residential and last two years. You should note that many applicants have higher qualifications; some will have A levels. The minimum age at entry is usually $17\frac{1}{2}$ to 18 years, but you can apply when you are 16. While waiting, you can improve your educational qualifications or get work experience. Most of the private nursery training colleges (see Further Information section) offer their own prestigious awards in addition to the NNEB Diploma. Local authorities have differing policies on whether to help with fees at these private colleges. Check carefully with your local authority.

Montessori qualifications

Various private organisations offer courses (full-time, part-time and correspondence) in the Montessori approach to working with small children. Some of these courses award teaching certificates and diplomas, but they may also be of interest to people wishing to work as nursery assistants. They are recognised only within the private sector of nursery schools and day nurseries, but there they have a good and growing reputation. The London Montessori Centre, for example, offers a number of courses, including a Certificate in Nannying and an Infant Toddler Teaching Diploma, which may be of particular interest. 'Montessori' nurseries can be found in many towns.

Julie – a qualified nursery nurse

Julie works in a private day nursery, which takes up to 20 children, from babies to school age.

My day starts early, as the nursery opens at 8.00am, when the parents drop off their children. So, things are busy from the start. There are four other qualified nursery staff, besides the manager. We all have to work closely together, planning out the day. My training showed me how important it is to give the children plenty of activities which help them to develop, and to become more independent. So the job is much more than just basic caring work – although there is plenty of routine work involved – helping with mealtimes, tidying, clearing up after the children, helping them put on their clothes if they go outside, changing babies' nappies and so on.

Much of our time is spent keeping the children active and happy. I usually have a small group of children to supervise. I organise group activities and games. I also make sure I give each child plenty of individual attention. Storytelling, singing, helping the children to paint a picture or to make something are all part of my working day. Making sure that the children are learning to communicate, and encouraging them to talk, is also important.

We have to be very careful about health and safety, of course. We also get to know the children well, and keep a check on their health and development.

To be a good nursery nurse, you need to love being with children – even when they are feeling fretful! You need plenty of patience, stamina and sensitivity. You need to be creative, and have plenty of imagination. It's a rewarding job. And it'll give me the opportunity to travel – I'm planning to spend a period working as a nursery nurse in Canada sometime in the future.

FINDING EMPLOYMENT

Job opportunities in local authority day and residential nurseries or hospitals are mainly for trained and qualified nursery nurses. In recent years there has been an increase in the number of private day nurseries and nursery schools. Private establishments vary in their requirements, and may employ a mixture of qualified staff as nursery nurses, and unqualified assistants. Those that accept you on the basis of your experience and personality may offer opportunities to gain qualifications within the job, such as NVQs in Child Care and Education or in Playwork.

Jobs for nursery nurses are generally advertised in the local press or in national publications such as *The Lady*, the *Times Educational Supplement* and *Nursery World*. Some recruitment agencies specialise in jobs for nannies and nursery nurses in private families, and there are many openings abroad as well as in the UK.

NANNY, PARENT'S HELP & AU PAIR

> The job of caring for children in a family setting is very varied. You could work as a full-time live-in nanny, as a part-time childcarer during the day, or as an au pair employed for a limited period. There are no specific entry requirements – while some employers prefer someone with childcare qualifications, others will look for the right personality.

Every job is different, and a lot depends upon the employer – their lifestyle and social status, whether or not both parents work, whether they live in the city or the country, whether they employ other staff, whether they treat you as 'staff' or 'family', and the number and ages of the children.

Many families are excellent employers and provide all sorts of perks – your own bathroom, TV, holidays abroad, the use of a car (a driving licence is sometimes a requirement of the job). Other employers may try to get all the work they can from you, for very little pay or thanks!

Fitting in
Your employer's ways may be very different from yours. Working alone for a large part of the day can be a lonely life. You need to be self-reliant, mature and responsible. This is especially true of working abroad as an au pair, where you may also have to struggle with language and cultural differences.

Looking after children in private families is open to both males and females, and posts are not normally exempt from the sex discrimination legislation. Because of the lifestyle, these are jobs mainly for the younger single person, and rarely a long-term career. If live-in family jobs become inappropriate, you can move into day nursery work, if you have suitable qualifications. (See section on working in private households, below.)

Nanny

Nannies often work for reasonably well-off families where both parents work. The nanny typically has sole charge of the child or children for at least part of the day, and is often also expected to do some light cleaning and cooking for the children. Hours are often irregular, and can therefore affect your social life. Most jobs are live-in, though there is an increasing demand for daily and even part-time or shared nannies.

TRAINING

You don't have to be qualified to work as a nanny, but many employers demand a nursery nursing diploma, or similar qualification. Some even specify particular colleges (e.g. Norland). Most want nannies aged at least 18, and often over 20, especially if there is a young baby in the family. Good qualifications will help you to get the best-paid jobs. Families often also expect driving skills, swimming and sometimes riding. Non-smoking is often specified.

You can train as a nursery nurse at a private college, or at a college of further education. A full list of colleges running Council for Awards in Children's Care and Education courses can be obtained by sending a stamped self-addressed A4 envelope to CACHE at the address in the Further Information section.

Further education colleges also offer a range of health and care-related courses leading to GNVQ and BTEC qualifications. The London Montessori Centre offers a Certificate in Nannying.

Parents' help

Many jobs involve living-in, though some families prefer to employ help on a daily basis. As a parent's help you would probably assist with all household jobs – cleaning, washing and ironing, cooking and washing up. You would also help to look after any children and babies, though, unlike a nanny, you would not usually be in sole charge. You would get them bathed, dressed and fed; take them for walks; play with them and read to them; take them to school, and so on. You might be responsible for cooking their meals, washing their clothes, cleaning and tidying their toys.

TRAINING

No particular qualifications are required – it is entirely up to the family to decide who to employ. A good general education will help, and many families will expect your spoken English to be good. You could start straight from school, though families may prefer someone older. A health and care full-time college course would be a good preparation.

Once employed, the only training you are likely to receive is that given by the parents while you are working. You'll have to fit in with their ways of dealing with the children and household tasks. Sometimes a nanny will also be employed, and you would learn while helping them. You could then train as a nursery nurse, after some experience.

Au pair

Au pairs carry out very similar tasks, but they are meant to be a temporary member of the family, and should be given time off for leisure and study. Working as an au pair is by nature a 'fill-in' job, rather than a career.

FINDING A JOB

Vacancies for nannies and parent's helps are often advertised in *The Lady*, *Nursery World* or *Horse and Hound*. For local jobs, local papers and employment agencies are the best place to look. Most employment is in London and the South-East.

Agencies can help you find a post, and, if they place you, they should also be able to help you if problems arise. Private colleges often have their own registry of vacancies for their own students. Au pairs find posts either through personal contacts, privately placed adverts, or agencies. Agencies provide you with the best safeguards against exploitation. You should normally be aged 18 or over for posts overseas; work permits are not required for jobs in EU countries.

ACCEPTING A JOB

Make sure you are given a written contract of employment which makes clear your duties and the conditions of work (pay, hours, holidays, etc) and states both your responsibilities and those of the family which employs you. See that your employer arranges to pay tax and National Insurance on your behalf, if you are paid above the limit at which this applies.

WORKING IN PRIVATE HOUSEHOLDS

The heyday of domestic service is long gone, but there is still employment in private households, and certain jobs are actually on the increase. Not all the work is in very rich households either – some jobs are with families or individuals of quite modest means. Prior training may not be necessary.

Why work in a private household?

You may be attracted to this sort of work because you like the domestic tasks associated with childcare (cooking, housekeeping, cleaning). You may prefer the idea of working for a private family as opposed to working in a nursery or residential home – perhaps being interested in the lifestyle that often goes with jobs in private families, such as the availability of accommodation with the job, or the possibility of travelling abroad with the family.

Sex discrimination and private households

Until recently, employment in private households was exempt from the sex discrimination legislation. Employers were allowed to state if they wanted a man or a woman, married or unmarried. Now, however, there can no longer be any discrimination in employing someone to work in a private household, unless the job involves a certain amount of physical or social contact with someone in the family, or otherwise affects personal privacy.

TRAINING FOR WORK IN PRIVATE HOUSEHOLDS

Generally, the training required of staff depends to a great extent on the views of the employer. Some will require their househelp to have taken a formal training; others may prefer a person with practical experience gained through looking after their own family. Most of the training courses which are reasonably appropriate for people wishing to work in private households do not train their students just for that sort of work – they may also be preparing people to work in nurseries or residential homes, for instance.

What the work involves

Working as a home help or cleaner usually means spending just a couple of hours each day or week with one particular household. You agree things like your rate of pay and the duties you will combine with childcare for each employer. A **home help** would carry out a wider range of jobs than a nanny – you would probably do cleaning, cooking, ironing, etc. This might just be a part-time job, or you might work for a number of households and build up a full-time job for yourself. You would not be expected to have trained for this work – just to have the usual sort of experience of caring for children in your own home.

In Britain, **tutors** are generally only employed to give children extra tuition before important exams or in the school holidays, such as when they are home from boarding school. Full-time jobs in this country are very scarce, though you do see occasional adverts for posts abroad (e.g. in the *Times Educational Supplement* and *The Lady*, both published on Fridays). Most families would specify a fully-trained and experienced teacher for such posts.

CHILDMINDING & FOSTERING

Childminding and fostering involve looking after children in your own home. They are responsible, demanding jobs. Childminders must be licensed and aware of the regulations affecting their work. Foster-parents are very carefully selected by local social services departments.

Childminding and fostering both involve caring for children, but are very different jobs. **Childminders** look after other people's children during set hours, often because the parents are at work. **Foster-parents** will have a child, or children, living with them full-time as part of the family, for a period. Foster-children may come from disadvantaged backgrounds, or have special needs. Both jobs require people who gain great satisfaction from looking after children, and are concerned with children's welfare.

Childminding

There is a legal requirement to register as a childminder with the social services before you start to look after someone else's under-eight-year-old child for more than two hours a day, for payment. There are limits on the numbers of children you may legally look after in your home at any one time – you should check these with your local social services department.

As a childminder, you must provide a safe and stimulating home environment for the child, including giving meals if the period of minding covers mealtimes. No formal educational qualifications are needed, but you would be expected to have a mature outlook towards childcare. It is possible to get NVQs in Child Care and Education. Social services departments will send information leaflets to people interested in childminding and encourage them to attend pre-registration meetings in their area.

Legal requirements must be fulfilled and, subject to meeting these (your home, health and any police records are checked), you will be approved and placed on a register which every local authority social services department keeps. Childminders are self-employed and set their own fees. The National Childminding Association can advise on what to charge, and on other financial matters. Each registered childminder is reviewed annually to see that standards are kept up. In some areas, specialist childminders are employed to look after children with particular needs.

You can become a member of the National Childminding Association and join a local support group. Some groups invite speakers to talk on topics such as the Red Cross, the role of health visitors and equal opportunities, so that childminders are kept up to date.

This is a way of earning money while you are looking after your own child, but you need to consider the wear and tear on your home and the effect that it might have on your own children. You will become involved not only with the children you care for, but with their parents too, and a working relationship must be developed with them. They are paying for your service, so they will feel they have a right to expect good standards of care, cooperation and reliability.

Fostering

There are many reasons why a child may be placed in a foster-home – perhaps the mother has to go into hospital and there is no one to look after the children, or the parent of a child with disabilities might want a break. Children in these cases would be fostered on a short-term basis and would go home as soon as possible.

If a child, of any age, cannot return to their own home – for example, where parents are unable to look after them, or where the court decides that the parents are not fit to look after them – long-term fostering is sought. Unlike in adoption, foster-children are still legally members of their own families. Even if the child is not expected to return home, some contact may be kept up with parents or relatives.

Fostering is under the control of the local social services department, which tries very hard to place the right child with the right family. Although fostering is open to all people – single or married, men and women – in practice married couples make up the largest proportion of foster-carers. They do not necessarily need to have had children themselves. Very often it is the couple whose own offspring have grown up and left who find that they have the time and resources to offer a child a secure and happy home.

What it takes

The qualities needed to be a good foster-carer are:

- a great capacity for giving love and care to children;
- an understanding of their needs – every child is an individual;
- tolerance – foster-carers need an awareness of cultural, religious and social factors, and of the needs of the child's parents;
- patience – foster-children away from their family may be distressed and need extra understanding;
- the ability to say goodbye to a child they have loved, and even to help the child's parents to be ready to accept the child back.

How do you become a foster-carer?

There are no official training schemes or specific qualification requirements, but that does not mean that everyone applying to be a foster-carer will be accepted. An interview is set up between the prospective family and the social worker (the whole family is involved, not just adults), and there will be some form-filling to do. Other interviews follow, and checks are made with the health authorities, the police and the NSPCC. All this is done to ensure the child is not put at any risk.

Information and training sessions are set up for groups of potential foster-carers, by the end of which they should know what fostering is all about and whether they are suited to it as a family.

Once an application is successful and a child has been placed in the home, the foster-carer will have support from social services. Every child and carer has their contact to help and support them. Some foster-carers have formed support groups to share problems and help each other.

Although allowances are made to foster-carers, raising a child is an expensive business. The allowance should cover your expenses, but there are no big profits to be made. Foster-carers of children with special needs can receive extra allowances to cover the increased costs.

just
THE
JOB

PLAYWORKER

Playworkers are part of a team which provides opportunities for children's play in different ways and different settings. Their role is similar to that of youth workers, but playworkers are associated with a younger age group, usually from about five to 15 years. Playworkers may lead a project and work directly with children, or be an area organiser for a group of projects. Generally, you don't need particular academic qualifications to begin this work, unless you want to make a study of playwork at higher education level.

Many jobs are based in adventure playgrounds, but there is a steadily increasing range of opportunities in playcentres, community projects, hospital children's wards, play buses and after-school clubs. There are also holiday care schemes. Work with under-school-age children is usually done by childcare workers in toddler groups and playgroups.

What the work involves

The work involves creating an environment which supports children's creative, imaginative, social and physical play. This means organising materials and equipment and keeping basic records, accounts and registers. A playcentre may offer indoor activities (arts and crafts, music, drama, etc) and an outside play area for building dens and treehouses, lighting camp-fires, digging, climbing, swimming. Trips and visits outside may also be arranged. Playworkers try to provide a relaxed atmosphere and, apart from safety, there should be few restrictions.

Playworkers are busiest at weekends and in school holidays. Hours may not be regular, but the basic pattern might be: term time weekdays 3.30 pm–6.00 pm (and sometimes before school too); weekends and holidays 10.00 am–6.00 pm, or sometimes later.

Rose – playworker

I have been a playworker for about three years now and, although I started as a volunteer when I was doing my GCSEs at school, I now have a paid job – employed part-time by the local council to run a holiday playscheme for children aged five to 14 years.

To start with, I only volunteered to help out two evenings a week with the after-school club. I was considering whether to apply for training as a sick children's nurse, and knew I'd need some experience with children across the whole age range. I'm an only child, and I hadn't had first-hand experience of children's natural development and linked interests – only my own and my friends'. I was rather shy and self-conscious with the children to start with, but as I got to know their individual personalities, that soon wore off!

I found that I was organising games and joining in, and yelling for the losing team with the best of them. I have developed lots of creative skills, trying to find attractive craft-work projects, or activities where you get something useful as an end-result. I like to chat to the children and now they tell me all about their latest interests, their homes and friends. Some of them do have problems, sometimes big ones, sometimes little ones which I can help them to solve. I suppose that, sometimes, they find it easier to relate to someone who is not quite an adult.

We have a number of different voluntary workers at the after-school club, but a smaller, more constant number of men and women for the holiday playscheme. One or two fellow-playworkers are students at the same stage as me – taking their A levels. We compare notes, and I think we have all been surprised by how much we have enjoyed doing this job. Of course, it can be tiring, even exhausting some days, but there is great pleasure and satisfaction in seeing the young people learning new activities and feeling proud of their own achievements. Most of these kids would be on the street for a large part of the day if they didn't spend time in the playscheme, so I feel that as well as learning to mix and take part in activities with others, they are safer and better occupied.

I feel much more determined to do a degree in nursing now that I can see a fulfilling career route stretching ahead. I have gained so much self-confidence and, dare I say, maturity, as a playworker!

Who employs playworkers?

Playworkers are employed by various voluntary groups and local authorities. Permanent playgrounds with playworkers are mostly found in larger cities. Many other towns provide temporary summer playschemes. The Playlink organisation provides play-work training and advice. There are approximately 200 perma-nent adventure playgrounds in England and Wales.

Each centre has at least two playworkers, but the total number in paid employment is very small. Some local authorities recruit temporary staff, including students, to run summer playschemes; some are run on a voluntary basis. Jobs are advertised in *New Statesman and Society*, *Times Educational Supplement*, *Youth Service*, in the local papers, and sometimes in the national press – especially the *Guardian*.

HAPA is an organisation which offers children with disabilities the chance to be stretched and challenged in play as much as more physically-able children. They run six play sites in London and a national information and training service.

TRAINING

Two-year full-time Diploma in Higher Education in Playwork is offered at Leeds Metropolitan University, the University of Northumbria and Thurrock College (through the University of East London). Entry is by a wide variety of qualifications and/or experience. The first year of this course is also offered at Norton College, Sheffield; students then take the second year at Leeds. Other institutions may also offer the course in future: check with the ECCTIS database and higher education handbooks.

Part-time/in-service courses in playwork are offered at various colleges of further education. There is a Playwork Foundation course, aimed at workers in out-of-school clubs and centres, which is a good basis from which to go on to achieve NVQs. Information about the course can be obtained from Kids Club Network. The National Centre for Playwork Education offer an introductory course 'Take Ten for Play', and Play-Train provide training in various aspects of playwork with a particular interest in equal opportunities, creative play and children's rights.

NVQs in Playwork at levels 2 to 4 can be achieved. Details about their availability nationwide can be obtained from one of the four National Centres for Playwork Education and Training. City & Guilds, CACHE, RSA, BTEC and SQA are all awarding bodies for NVQs in Playwork, from whom further information can be obtained.

WORKING IN RESIDENTIAL CHILDCARE

Residential childcare can involve working in homes and nurseries run by local authorities and charities. You might be looking after children with special educational needs or those who have been taken into care. You must be over 18 to start working, and to start training you will need at least a few good GCSEs.

What the work involves

There are many reasons why children find themselves living in residential homes, rather than with their own families:

- some children have parents who cannot or will not look after them;
- some will have suffered neglect or abuse by their families;
- there are children with learning difficulties or physical disabilities which mean that their parents are not able to care for them at home;
- some children may have broken the law and been put into care by a court order.

Many of the children in residential care are in some way disadvantaged in life. Some are unhappy and disturbed, and some may be coping with disabilities. This means that life is not easy for them, nor for the people who are looking after them. These children need to get at least some of the things they will miss through not having an ordinary home life. They need not just physical care, food and clothes, but love, trips to the seaside, help in looking after themselves – all the things you hardly think about if you come from an ordinary family home.

Residential homes include reception centres, where children stay while assessments and future plans are made; small family-type homes; nurseries and larger homes, some of which are for groups of children with special needs. The homes are run both by local authorities and by private charities. Part of the work of children's homes is to help children and their families either by trying to reunite them, or by arranging fostering or adoption. Most children do not remain for long periods in a home.

There is more need for staff in towns than in country areas. The social services department of your local authority will know what residential homes there are in your area. As well as local authority homes, there are homes and centres run by voluntary agencies like Barnardo's and NCH Action for Children, which sometimes offer jobs. Similar work may also be found in privately-run or local authority boarding schools – including those for children with special needs. Your local education authority will be able to give you addresses.

What it takes

It is not enough just to like children and to enjoy being with them. You need to:

■ be prepared to work with children who are disturbed, frustrated or demanding;
■ be able to understand the children's difficulties and problems;
■ be patient and tolerant;
■ have stamina – a sense of humour also helps;
■ work as part of a team;
■ be prepared to do shift work, and work overnight – perhaps on a rota system.

TRAINING

There are various college courses which could prepare you for working with children in residential care. These include

GNVQ and BTEC and nursery nursing courses. Educational requirements vary, but nursery nursing courses usually ask for three GCSEs at grade C.

National Vocational Qualifications are available for anyone already working in residential childcare. These awards are based on assessments of competence in the workplace. NVQs are designed to allow people to progress at their own pace, giving credit for skills gained.

The minimum age of entry is eighteen years, and suitable mature applicants are welcomed. If you are a school-leaver, it could be worth taking one of the courses mentioned to give you a taste of the work, as well as the knowledge and maturity to survive once you start working. A further way of getting experience is to become a **volunteer helper** with a local organisation.

Diploma in Social Work (DipSW)

People already working in residential care or a related area can take the Diploma in Social Work (DipSW), the professional qualification for social workers in the United Kingdom, as a college-based course, or as an employment-based programme – see the next section.

SOCIAL WORK

Social workers try to help individuals and families with all manner of problems, the roots of which may lie in illness, unemployment, poor housing, low income or old age. Helping people to come to terms with – or to solve – their problems is not an easy job. A social worker therefore needs a good education, followed by professional training, and the right personality.

Different types of social work

Social work can be either voluntary or paid. Voluntary work offers scope for many different activities, including meals on wheels for local elderly people; providing hospital cars; taking disabled children swimming; and work overseas in developing countries.

Paid social work can be done at professional or assistant level, and is the main focus of this section. Most social workers are employed by local authority social services departments, but there are also opportunities for employment with charities and other organisations.

Social workers are employed within all types of communities, not just in run-down inner cities, and have dealings with people of all types, ages and backgrounds – children, elderly people, families and single parents. Every case is different.

Nowadays, most social workers specialise in a particular type of work. They may concentrate on:

- cases involving young children, adoptions and fostering arrangements;
- people who are mentally or physically ill;
- work in residential homes for children and young people who cannot live with their natural families;
- an increasing amount of community care work with elderly and disabled people who might previously have lived in hospitals or residential homes.

Other social workers are **education welfare officers**, dealing with any problems which may prevent schoolchildren from getting the most out of their educational opportunities. Present **probation officers** are qualified social workers who specialised in working with young offenders and prisoners, and also in working towards the rehabilitation of people who have served prison sentences.

Besides those jobs which actually need qualified social workers, there are many other situations which are closely related to social work: **youth workers** working with young people from ethnic minorities; **careers officers** who choose to specialise in work with youngsters with special needs; **community workers**; **play leaders**; **health visitors**; **church workers**, to give some examples. For fuller details about these, see the relevant sections in this book.

Satisfactions and drawbacks

Many people want to do some kind of social work because of a desire to help people in difficulties, but they do not always realise what a hard job it is. Social workers have rules and guidelines to follow in dealing with problems, but there may be no simple solutions to the situations which they meet. They often have to rely on their own initiative and on techniques learned during training. In some cases, there may be no long-term solution at all to a problem. Lack of funds, or a client's refusal to cooperate, may mean that an obvious route to solving a problem can't be followed. Then, the social worker's efforts come to nothing.

Much of social work is about helping people to cope with continuing problems, rather than finding a magical cure. Some clients can be uncooperative, ungrateful and even violent, and the social worker who thinks he or she is going to change the world and solve every problem will be disappointed! People often regard social workers as interfering do-gooders, or as ineffective people who ignore things like early-warning signals of child abuse. It's a very hard job to get right, and social workers often receive a lot of criticism. But there are many satisfactions too.

Not just client-contact ...

Remember that, although it is very much a people-based job, there is also a lot of paperwork and administration to be carried out. There are records to keep, and liaison with other organisations such as the Department of Social Security, the police, community workers and the education services. The social worker is often a go-between. Sometimes, this means negotiating on behalf of the client – perhaps with the police, or to get welfare benefits, or in dealing with a housing problem. But social workers themselves also become involved in legal procedures. They may have to take children into care – often against the wishes of the parents – and have to assist in the interpretation of the Mental Health Act when arrangements are being made for the compulsory admission of mentally ill patients to hospital. There are also court appearances, when they give social reports on offenders.

What it takes

The work can be emotionally demanding. You must be able to appreciate your clients' problems without getting involved on a personal basis. You have to be tough enough and tolerant enough to put up with occasional abuse and lack of cooperation

from clients, whilst still carrying on trying to help them. You also have to be very observant and not easily taken in. Headline reports of cases of severe child abuse show up the awful results which can occur when social workers and other professionals do not recognise that all is not well with a child under their supervision.

As problems do not arise only during office hours, social workers often have to work in the evenings and at weekends. You may be expected to be able to drive – if you can't, you'll certainly find that your choice of jobs is restricted.

PROFESSIONAL QUALIFICATIONS AND TRAINING

The Diploma in Social Work (DipSW) is the professional qualification for all social workers in the United Kingdom, in whatever setting or sector they work. DipSW programmes require at least two years of full-time study, or the part-time equivalent, and supervised practice. The DipSW can be taken through a course of college-based training or via an employment-based route. Employment-based students are already employed in social services when they apply for admission to a programme. Admission is with the agreement of the employer. Students keep their jobs and continue to be paid a salary. The majority of DipSW students train through college-based programmes.

Students may choose to follow either a general pathway, or a particular pathway which gives the opportunity to specialise in a specific group of clients or kind of service.

There are different types of DipSW programmes to cater for graduates, school-leavers and college-leavers with A levels or equivalent and non-graduates. Most DipSW programmes are full-time, but some offer part-time options and some are extended to make it easier for people with family commitments to undertake training. Distance-learning routes are also available. About half of all entrants to social work courses are non-graduate, but many of these will be older entrants. If you are still at school or college and wondering which is the best route to take, note that promotion prospects are likely to be better with a degree. The route chosen will also depend on how committed you are to the idea of a social work career – obviously a degree keeps alternative career options open.

Degree programmes combined with DipSW
Various universities and colleges of higher education offer programmes leading to both a degree and DipSW qualification. These programmes last for three to four years. These are the most relevant for school-leavers and college-leavers with a strong commitment to social work, but they are also appropriate to older applicants who are suitably qualified. Relevant work experience is usually required. Application is through UCAS.

Non-graduate DipSW programmes

These are two-year programmes which are often combined with a Diploma of Higher Education (DipHE). Applications for most full-time programmes are through the Social Work Admissions System (SWAS) – apply from September for programmes beginning a year later. There are also some part-time and extended programmes for non-graduates; applications for these are sent direct to the institution concerned.

Postgraduate DipSW courses

If you already have a degree, or want to take a degree before making any firm commitment to a social work career, this is the route for you. Relevant work experience is required. Some programmes require a social science degree, but many institutions will accept a good degree in any subject. In exceptional cases, non-graduates with very substantial experience or other further education or professional qualifications may be considered. Postgraduate DipSW programmes last for two years. Candidates with a relevant degree may be able to negotiate credit exemptions with the programme. Some bursaries are available, although not for students wishing to specialise in education welfare work. You can obtain further information from CCETSW. Application is through SWAS.

Note: it is important to check that a DipSW programme is approved by the Central Council for Education and Training in Social Work (CCETSW).

ENTRY REQUIREMENTS

An applicant to a DipSW programme must, in the opinion of the programme provider, be likely to succeed in completing the programme and be suitable person to become a social worker.

All candidates under the age of 21 must have a minimum of two A levels plus supporting GCSEs at grade C. Equivalent qualifications would be a relevant BTEC National

Diploma/Certificate, Advanced GNVQ or NVQ level 3. Certain Open University courses, or Access course qualifications, or a Nursery Nursing diploma may also be accepted as entry requirements. Universities will often require three A levels. The DipSW cannot be awarded to candidates under 22.

Candidates over the age of 21 are not required to have formal qualifications, but will be expected to demonstrate their ability to study at an advanced level.

Most DipSW programmes require candidates to have had work experience in social services or a related field. A minimum of one year's experience of either paid or voluntary work is often required, and the majority of successful applicants to social work training have between two and five years' experience.

PROSPECTS FOR SOCIAL WORKERS

A recent survey shows that demand for newly qualified social workers is high. Most students have the promise of a job before they qualify – often in the locality where they trained. Jobs in community care are on the increase, while residential care is decreasing. To see the sorts of vacancies which arise for new and experienced social workers, look at the job adverts in the *Guardian* on Wednesdays – which you can buy, or read in your public library – also in *Community Care* and *Care Weekly*. Promotion prospects for experienced social workers are quite good, but, as in many professions, senior posts normally involve more management responsibility and less casework.

Once you have your basic social work qualification, you can go on to study for post-qualifying awards in specialist areas of work, such as family therapy and childcare law.

just THE JOB

YOUTH WORK

Youth workers help young people to develop their skills and qualities to the full, both as individuals and as members of society. Youth work may be done voluntarily or as paid employment. Professional youth workers have usually had previous experience as a volunteer, or as a part-time worker.

Usually, young people get involved with the youth service to meet friends, to get out of the home for a while, to take part in some special activity, or to get help with a particular problem. Youth workers work with different age groups – the youth service is open to all young people aged between 11 and 26, with a special emphasis on the 13–19 group.

Youth workers are employed mainly by local authority education departments. There are also opportunities in projects concerned with information, advice and counselling for young people, or with voluntary organisations such as the clubs run full-time by the YMCA or YWCA. The majority of youth work in Britain is part-time, so full-time jobs can be difficult to find. It is worth considering getting a degree or qualification for a broader occupational area, or different job, before starting youth work training.

Youth work in clubs and centres

It isn't easy to define youth work in clubs and centres. Youth workers respond in a variety of ways to the needs of young people as they pass through adolescence to adulthood. The emphasis of the work in a particular post will depend on a number of factors, such as the social structure of the community and whether it is located in a rural or urban area.

What the work involves

The work can include: organising activities to challenge young people in various ways, such as taking part in the Duke of Edinburgh's Award scheme; organising social and sporting activities for club members; working with unemployed young people; organising events away from the club premises; administering and managing the finances of the club; dealing with structural maintenance and general upkeep of the centre; recruiting and training voluntary workers; assisting and advising at smaller clubs which do not have a professional worker; liaising with professional and voluntary groups interested in the welfare of young people; individual counselling of young people; encouraging the involvement of young people in their community; organising international exchanges of young people; marketing the use of the club/centre facilities, locally – perhaps by other groups; and assessing and responding to the leisure requirements of young people in the area.

Youth and community work in other settings

Many youth workers operate outside youth centres in order to reach young people who choose not to make use of clubs. Jobs include:

- youth work posts in the leisure industry, which may be based in a youth centre, a wing of a school or a sports centre;
- 'detached' youth work – i.e. working with young people who, for one reason or another, are not in contact with other agencies. Workers have to make themselves available in the places where these young people go – in cafes, pubs and on the streets;
- youth social work, in local authority social services departments. This may involve setting up community-based care

for young people at risk of becoming seriously involved in criminal activity;
- helping young unemployed people to occupy their time usefully;
- young volunteer organisers – assisting young people who want to do voluntary work in the community;
- joint teacher/youth work jobs, often called 'youth tutor' posts, and others which carry responsibility for adult education as well as youth work, e.g. in community centres.

What it takes

Youth workers come from a wide variety of backgrounds, and their personalities can be just as varied. It helps if you can relate to both young people and adults, and here good listening and communication skills are essential. As a youth worker you'll need plenty of initiative and enthusiasm to get projects started, and any interest in sport or outdoor activities, art or music is a bonus. There are always some administrative tasks to take care of – principally, managing resources and staff. In this work you'll be busy on certain evenings and sometimes at weekends, which will definitely affect your social and family life.

TRAINING

For most full-time posts with local education authorities, and also with many voluntary organisations, it is necessary to have a qualification recognised by the National Youth Agency. There are some posts for unqualified youth workers, but such opportunities are extremely limited.

The content of the different types of youth work training courses varies. Applicants should study prospectuses carefully to find the most appropriate courses for their needs. Special interests can be pursued, such as working with young unemployed people, or youth work in multicultural settings. All courses involve a large amount of practical work with placements in youth clubs.

Courses acceptable to the National Youth Agency
Certificate or Diploma in Youth & Community Work (two years) – five GCSEs at grade C (or the equivalent) are the usual minimum entry requirement, although all colleges are prepared to consider applicants with lower qualifications if they have had relevant experience. Except where stated, the minimum entry age is 21. Contact the NYA for a current list of courses offered.

Postgraduate courses for holders of any degree – competition for places is severe and relevant part-time or voluntary experience will greatly assist. The NYA will provide information on the availability of courses.

DipHE/first degrees – there are several courses in youth and community work which are designated as DipHE (Diploma of Higher Education) or degree courses. Consult the *Compendium of Higher Education* for a list of the universities and colleges which have professional endorsement from the NYA.

Other recognised qualifications and training
There are also various other types of qualifications currently recognised as being equivalent to youth work training. The National Youth Agency considers applicants with such qualifications on an individual basis.

There is also an increasing number of part-time and distance-learning opportunities leading to professional qualifications. Further information can be obtained from the National Youth Agency.

EDUCATION WELFARE OFFICER

The education welfare officer's job is to make sure that all children benefit fully from education. They are really doing social work in an education setting, and are often called *education social workers*. The qualifications requested by employers vary, but the Diploma in Social Work is usually required.

Education welfare officers still have their traditional job of dealing with problems of non-attendance at school by children under the statutory school-leaving age, and, where necessary, they prosecute parents whose children persistently stay away from school. But, generally, their role is now much wider than this.

What the work involves

Education welfare officers are concerned with children whose family difficulties – which may be social, emotional or financial – give rise to behavioural problems or under-achievement at school. Generally, EWOs have responsibility for a school or group of schools in a particular neighbourhood.

- They make sure that families who should be getting help – such as free school meals, clothing, transport – receive such help.
- They try to develop better links between home and school, working closely with parents, teachers and school psychologists, and with other agencies such as the social services department, the probation service and the careers service.

- They may assist in making decisions concerning the provision of suitable education for children with special educational needs.

Though EWOs are backed up by the legal system, they try, by persuasion and encouragement, to convince reluctant (and possibly resistant!) parents and children of the advantages of full-time education.

What it takes

Education welfare officers need:

- to be able to deal tactfully and sympathetically with all types of adults and children;
- to be sensitive to people's problems;
- maturity;
- patience;
- perseverance;
- accurate record-keeping and report-writing skills.

Experience of working with people in a caring or supervisory role is very useful, as the work can be challenging and at times frustrating. However, the demands of the job are countered by the special rewards of working successfully with young people in difficulties.

QUALIFICATIONS AND TRAINING

Traditionally, education welfare has been a job for an older person, but increasingly, younger staff under 25 are being appointed. Where an authority does not insist on social work qualifications, there are opportunities for people from a wide variety of backgrounds, including teaching, but different local authorities tend to emphasise different requirements.

For information on the Diploma in Social Work (DipSW), see the section on social work, above.

CONDITIONS OF EMPLOYMENT

EWOs do not have a fixed working week. Hours can be both long and unsocial. There will be evening work and weekend work to do – visiting parents who are out during the day. Overtime payments may be made for this. The holiday entitlement is approximately four weeks plus public holidays – it varies according to the grade of the post and length of service. During school holidays, EWOs carry out normal casework as well as the administrative work related to their duties.

PROSPECTS

Within education welfare itself, promotion prospects are not very great, because of the relatively small number of staff employed in each local authority. However, there are higher-grade posts for senior and principal education welfare officers. To take full advantage of promotion prospects, it would be necessary to move to other parts of the country as jobs arose. Pay is comparable to other types of social work.

It is also possible to move into related occupations – such as the social services, youth service, careers service, probation service or education administration. Entry to these occupations depends upon the required academic and/or professional qualifications being held, but education welfare officers holding the DipSW would be in a better position for transfer to related social work jobs. As some of these services are larger in terms of the staff they employ, promotion prospects could be increased in this way.

EDUCATIONAL PSYCHOLOGIST

Psychologists study *what* people and animals do and investigate, by scientific means, *why* they do it. They use their understanding of behaviour to help solve people's problems and worries, and to improve the quality of their lives. To become a psychologist, you need a degree.

Psychologists investigate such things as:

- how children learn to speak their language;
- how humans and animals learn new skills;
- what motivates humans and animals to acquire new skills;
- why people, including close relatives, have different personalities;
- how people 'get on' with each other – how they interact;
- how drugs, such as alcohol and psychiatric drugs, affect behaviour;
- how people behave in groups and crowds.

A knowledge of psychology could be a valuable basis for a career in many fields, including social work, advertising and market research, personnel work, police work, journalism, careers advisory work and the probation service. Specialised training for these occupations can be undertaken after obtaining a degree. Probably less than a quarter of psychology graduates are employed as psychologists.

Where psychologists work

The British Psychological Society has a membership of about 28,000, including student members. Central government is one of the largest individual employers, with a staff of over 250. Many psychologists, including educational psychologists, are employed by local authorities.

Educational psychologist

Educational psychologists are concerned with the psychological and educational development of children and young people in the home, at school and in the community. They investigate learning, behaviour and emotional difficulties in children and young people and advise teachers, parents and others on ways of helping their clients. Posts are usually located in the psychological services department of a local education authority. They contribute to the work of other organisations, such as child guidance clinics and social service observation and assessment centres.

HOW TO BECOME A PSYCHOLOGIST

The normal first step towards a career as a professional psychologist is to take an honours degree (BA or BSc) in psychology. Courses are offered by almost all universities, including, on a part-time basis, the Open University, and by some colleges. Ensure that the degree course which you choose to follow has been approved by the British Psychological Society, as giving the Graduate Basis for Registration. This is a necessary prerequisite to becoming Registered as a Chartered Psychologist following accredited postgraduate professional training. If you take a degree course in a different subject, it is possible to obtain membership of the British Psychological Society by taking a one-year full-time, or two-year part-time, accredited conversion course, or by taking the Society's Qualifying Examination.

Psychology graduates who go on to take accredited postgraduate training in a specific area of psychology are entitled to register with the British Psychological Society as Chartered Psychologists. Qualification as a Chartered Psychologist is becoming an essential requirement for many posts in psychology.

Getting on a degree course in psychology

At least two A levels, but preferably three, are required to enter a degree course in psychology. Universities are likely to ask for high A level grades. Subject requirements vary from place to place. Suitable A level subjects include mathematics and biology, but arts and social science subjects are also appropriate. A level psychology is not required. Most courses require GCSE at grade C in mathematics. Some courses require GCSEs in double science at grade C. AS levels/Advanced GNVQ/BTEC National Diploma may be accepted as alternative entry qualifications. You should check the requirements of individual courses on the ECCTIS database, in higher education handbooks, or with the prospectuses of individual establishments.

TRAINING

Educational psychologists need to have completed a Postgraduate Certificate in Education, plus two years' teaching experience followed by a postgraduate training in educational psychology – usually a year, leading to a Master's degree and a year of supervised practice. Alternatively, qualified teachers can take a psychology degree part-time and then go on to the postgraduate course. Another route for non-psychology graduates is to take a one-year full-time accredited conversion course in psychology.

just THE JOB

COUNSELLING

When people feel they have a problem or are unhappy with some aspect of their lives, they might seek the help of a counsellor. Problems may involve experiencing distress, having a difficult decision to make, or a crisis to face. In private, and in confidence, counsellors help people to clarify and understand their problems, and find ways of meeting, or addressing, their needs.

What is counselling?

It is much easier to say what counselling is not, than to say what it is. It does *not* mean sitting in judgment on other people, or persuading them to follow a particular course of action, or giving advice ('*If I were you* ...'). Counselling takes place through a two-way relationship between the counsellor and the client. The counsellor helps clients to talk about their problem, getting to the root of it by listening to what they say, and asking questions which may probe deeper into certain issues relating to the problem. This will enable clients to learn about themselves, to assist them to find ways of getting to grips with the problem, and to develop as human beings.

Perhaps the client is a child who is very unhappy at home, and not doing well at school. Perhaps it's someone with an alcohol problem, or a teenage girl who is pregnant and under pressure from her family to have an abortion. Maybe it's a student who is unable to cope with the pressure of exams.

Where do counsellors work?

Counsellors work in a variety of settings, including schools, colleges, universities, etc, as well as special services or agencies set up to deal with specific types of problems. Full-time jobs for counsellors tend to be in educational settings, in workplace staff-counselling services and within the National Health Service. Other opportunities, especially outside large cities, are more likely to be part-time or voluntary activities.

Counsellors may work with their clients on the whole range of problems which they present. On the other hand, they may decide to refer a client to a more specialised source of help if that seems appropriate. Some counsellors become specialists in particular types of problem – e.g. in marriage guidance, bereavement, AIDS, drugs or alcohol-abuse counselling; or with a certain age range, especially teenagers and young adults.

What it takes

A counsellor is someone who:

- readily establishes a good relationship with people;
- is capable of listening carefully, interpreting what the person is saying sensitively;
- can, on occasions, infer what a person is *not* saying;
- is able to gain the complete trust of a client;
- is patient and tolerant and does not pass judgement or offer personal advice;
- is in touch with the client, understanding and seeing things from the client's point of view;
- is a sensitive and stable person;
- has a high level of self-awareness, knowing what personal resources to offer the client.

Counselling is not a career for a very young person. Considerable maturity is needed and, while some younger people might use counselling skills in their particular profession, it would be very unusual for people to enter full-time counselling work before their mid-twenties.

TRAINING

Because counselling is a 'second' career, people wishing to work in counselling will almost always first gain professional qualifications and experience in a related area of work. The most obviously-related occupational areas are teaching, careers advisory work, psychology, psychotherapy, youth and community work, the creative therapies such as drama therapy and art therapy, church work and social/probation work. Medical and health professions also give rise to opportunities for counselling. Many people enter counselling after working in the voluntary sector.

There is a broad range of training available in counselling, with a mixture of long, short, full-time and part-time courses being offered. Some courses are geared towards a particular type of counselling role – e.g. educational counselling, church work, careers guidance, bereavement help or marriage guidance.

Courses are offered by many types of providers, including universities, local colleges of further education, private training organisations and bodies such as Relate (marriage guidance) and the National Childbirth Trust. People wishing to work as school counsellors will almost certainly be expected to be qualified teachers with substantial teaching experience.

Courses include:

- full-time and part-time masters' degrees (such as MEd and MA) and certificate/diploma courses in guidance, counselling and related subjects. These are 'long' courses for professionally qualified people.
- various short courses (ranging from a few days to a term or more), both full-time and part-time, in aspects of counselling.

Some short courses have specific entry requirements, such as qualified teacher status; others are more flexible and may be suitable for voluntary workers. Some courses are geared very specifically to the needs of the organisations running them – e.g. Relate or specific young persons' counselling services. It would be worth contacting your local college of further education to see what kind of short courses are on offer; there may well be something, at least at an introductory level.

Accreditation by the British Association for Counselling (BAC) requires evidence of counselling practice and supervision by an experienced counsellor, so practical experience in counselling work must accompany theoretical training.

A comprehensive directory of recognised training courses in counselling and psychotherapy can be obtained from BAC (see Further Information section).

just
THE
JOB

CAREERS ADVISORY WORK

C areers advisers help people to make decisions about their education, training and future career. This is often called *vocational guidance*. Careers advisers work in local careers service companies, in schools, colleges and universities, in special guidance units for adults and in private vocational guidance agencies. You need to have a qualification in guidance and counselling to do this work, usually at a postgraduate level.

Careers adviser

Careers advisers aim to help clients to reach their own, well-informed decisions about their future. They do not *tell* people what to do or what job they are best suited to, but help to evaluate different courses of action and suggest opportunities for the client to consider.

Their work with individual clients involves interviewing them. This really means having a purposeful conversation – to establish what their abilities, preferences and priorities are. Therefore, careers advisers need to be good communicators, observant, and able to establish a relationship with people very quickly. An interest in psychology and human behaviour is important, together with an analytical mind and a good memory.

Careers advisers may use various tests and guides (often computer-based) to analyse people's interests, aptitudes and abilities. The results of these can improve the effectiveness of vocational guidance.

Besides being able to find out information about the client, the careers adviser must also know about educational, training and employment opportunities.

The careers service

Local careers service companies are the biggest employers of careers advisers, who can also be called *careers officers*. The basic task of advisers is to help school and college students and young unemployed people with their decisions and plans for the future, by providing free personal guidance and information. The service also helps young people to find suitable employment with training, and much of this work is handled by employment assistants or officers, working with careers advisers. There is also work with adults, particularly those in education or who have disabilities.

A careers adviser in a careers service spends a high proportion of the working week on casework – interviewing young people in local schools and colleges or at the careers centre, and perhaps talking to groups of young people with similar interests or with the same decisions to make. There is also report-writing and administration which has to be done in connection with casework. Many advisers use laptop computers for administrative work.

Time may also be spent seeing parents and, in some cases, liaising with training managers, college staff, personnel officers, social workers and other professionals. Discussions also take place with school and college staff, to agree a suitable level of provision for careers education and guidance.

Another major task is keeping up to date with local and national trends in education, employment and training – visiting local colleges, employers and those in employment with training, reading information items and researching particular topics from time to time. The careers adviser may also be involved in

organising occasional careers conventions, where young people and parents can meet representatives from education, training and industry.

PROSPECTS

After a couple of years doing the basic work, careers advisers may move into specialist areas, such as guidance for young people with special needs (learning difficulties or a physical disability, etc), employment and training liaison, information work, work with ethnic minorities or work with sixth formers and college students. There are also promoted posts which involve management responsibilities and supervision of staff, as well as senior management positions, with responsibility for running the careers service in an area. There is a one-year distance-learning package available which can lead to a Certificate in Management.

TRAINING

There are now two routes to becoming qualified as a careers adviser:

Assessment in the workplace for National Vocational Qualifications at level 3/4 in guidance work. The NVQs are suitable for those who are presently employed in related work within a careers service, or for those doing paid or unpaid voluntary work in counselling.

A full-time or part-time course at a university. This route is in two parts: a year of academic study followed by a year of approved employment and training. The first part involves taking a one-year full-time course, or a two-year part-time course, leading to a Diploma in Careers Guidance. Contact the Local Government Management Board for a list of course centres. There is also an open learning course available which can lead to the DipCG.

If you are under 25, you need to be a graduate, or near equivalent, to be accepted for a DipCG course. Older applicants, who are generally welcome, may offer other appropriate experience, for example in industry or teaching. Training awards from the Local Government Management Board are available to those who are over 25 and have been out of full-time education for more than two years. Some careers services take on trainees, paying them a salary during the course and offering them a job on completion. The LGMB can award a premium grant for in-service trainees.

Courses are followed by a first year in employment as a **probationer**, with on-the-job training and assessment in order to complete the qualification.

Other work in the careers service

Others employed by careers services include **employment assistants** (also called *associate advisers*), who liaise between young people and employers or trainers; **information assistants**; **receptionists** and **administrators**. These vacancies would be advertised locally.

It may also be possible to work in careers *information* without a DipCG but with relevant experience.

University and college careers services

Higher education establishments offer careers advice and help in finding vacancies for their students, most of whom are on degree and higher diploma courses. Besides the usual careers guidance functions – interviewing students, offering tests and providing information – careers advisers in higher education spend a large proportion of their time liaising with recruiters of graduates, and arranging meetings and interviews for final-year students to meet potential employers.

Many advisers in higher education have a background in industry, and vacancy advertisements (see the *Times Higher Education Supplement*) often specify that they want an adviser with a particular specialism, such as science or engineering. Some careers advisers have a DipCG and a previous background in a local careers service, but, though valuable, the Diploma is by no means essential for this type of work. Other qualifications in counselling or related areas may also prove useful.

School careers coordinator

Virtually all secondary schools (both state and private sector) have a **careers teacher** or **careers coordinator**, who is paid a special allowance for this responsibility. They may be promoted from within the school, or vacancies may be advertised in the usual places for teaching posts.

What careers teachers actually do varies considerably from one school to another. They may coordinate careers teaching and guidance activities, acting as an administrator or initiator, rather than an adviser. Others may actually do little beyond keeping a basic careers library. Occasionally, and perhaps mainly in the private sector, there are posts where the emphasis is on offering individual guidance to pupils and students.

Training for careers teachers is patchy – there are some one-year and one-term full-time courses available (for qualified teachers only). There are also a number of part-time in-service courses and basic short courses.

Private vocational guidance services and agencies

Some advisers work in private vocational guidance agencies. These may be one-person operations, or partnerships, and are generally based in the larger cities – especially in London and the South. Most agencies charge their clients quite substantial fees.

Careers advisers in private agencies tend to make extensive use of psychological tests. In fact, many advisers have a psychology background. Some may have higher education or local careers service experience, and may possess a Diploma in Careers Guidance. Occasionally, people employed elsewhere as careers advisers undertake some private work in addition to their salaried post.

Private agencies tend to offer a one-off, though in-depth, service to clients, which includes a programme of testing, a personal interview, and a written analysis and report which includes suggestions of career possibilities. There is little follow-up work and agencies do not generally provide an employment-placing service.

THE PROBATION SERVICE

The probation service, like the courts and the prison service, is part of the judicial system, and its work is backed up by the law. It has a supervisory role, representing the authority of the court, and, at the same time, it offers guidance and support to help offenders to redirect their lives. Professional training is given to people with relevant experience and qualifications.

What it takes

This might be a suitable job for you if you:

- are mature and well-balanced;
- can form relationships with people from all walks of life;
- can gain people's trust, and yet be authoritative when necessary;
- can work in the formal setting of a law court, and in prisons and youth custody centres;
- are prepared to take a demanding training course;
- are prepared to do a lot of report-writing for courts and prison parole boards;
- are willing to work in the evenings and at weekends;
- can drive and are willing to do a lot of travelling.

Working with people

Contrary to popular belief, most of the probation officer's work is not with young people, but with adults. They also work closely with other agencies, such as local authority social services departments, the Department of Social Security and voluntary bodies.

The most important skill that probation officers need is to be able to form personal relationships with offenders and others, many of whom may be very hostile and uncooperative. They must win trust and show that they care, yet be able also to exercise the authority of the legal system which they represent. It can be difficult to get this balance right.

Court orders and community work

Probation officers are concerned with offenders who are subject to court orders of various kinds. They supervise those offenders who have been placed under a probation order, for a fixed period of time, by the courts. Probation officers also supervise community service projects and day centres. They can be involved in victim support, sometimes mediating between offenders and their victims. They also try to provide 'preventive' care – encouraging interests and activities such as community work and outdoor pursuits, which may help to prevent past offenders from getting into further trouble by giving them a sense of purpose and of belonging.

In prison and after ...

With prisoners in detention, the probation officer's job is to help and advise them in all sorts of ways: sorting out family and marriage problems, and advising young offenders on education and training. A probation officer who works in a prison or other detention centre may be known as a **prison welfare officer**.

When prisoners leave custody, a probation officer will be involved in aftercare. In close liaison with the prison welfare officer, they supervise prisoners on parole, help ex-prisoners to find work and housing and to understand the benefits system, or find rehabilitation centres for those who have spent many years in prison and become 'institutionalised'.

Not just offenders

Although work with offenders is its major task, the probation service also deals with custody recommendations, and arrange-

62

ments for access where children are involved in divorce cases. This area of work calls for a high degree of tact and sensitivity.

GETTING STARTED

Probation officers no longer have to be qualified as social workers. New regulations are intended to encourage a wider range of mature candidates to apply for training, as attendance on a full-time diploma course is not required. Area probation services now recruit people directly, as salaried trainees.

Training and assessment is mainly carried out in the workplace, but with additional input from higher education institutions, as a considerable amount of background knowledge is required, as well as the specific skills gained through work experience. Previous qualifications, and experience gained in areas such as police work, social work or community work, will be taken into account, and may allow exemption from some of the training modules, which lead to a Diploma in Probation Studies.

Successful trainees are granted Qualified Probation Officer Status (QPOS), backed up by an NVQ at an appropriate level.

COMMUNITY WORK

Community workers provide facilities or advice, helping to solve problems on behalf of particular individuals or groups of people. They may work for a local authority – in the social services' department or in youth and community service: they may work for independent bodies, such as charities. Some jobs in community work require a degree; others ask for no particular academic qualifications.

The sorts of jobs which are described as *community work* include: **wardens of community centres** offering leisure and educational provision of all kinds for residents of a neighbourhood – old people, young people, housewives, unemployed people, etc; **youth and community workers** in youth clubs and centres – detached youth workers assist young people who, for one reason or another, are not involved with official youth organisations; **liaison officers** and advisers working in multi-racial communities; **playworkers** and playscheme organisers; people working for rural **community councils**; lawyers and other workers in **community law** centres; **counsellors** in young people's counselling and advisory services; **advisers** in housing advice centres; **community arts workers**, including artists, dramatists, musicians and administrators; and **students' welfare officers** – perhaps based in a university to help with problems of accommodation, the law, finance, etc.

Traditional community work

There are many opportunities to work for, with and within the community in the more traditional occupations, such as the police service (the community police officer on the beat), the health services (the district nurse, health visitor and community midwife), adult education, public libraries, and the churches. Some are covered elsewhere in this book, others in other books in the *Just the Job!* series, particularly *Care & Community*.

QUALIFICATIONS AND TRAINING

It is very difficult to generalise about qualifications and training for community work. Some posts may require no academic qualifications or formal training, while for others – e.g. in law advice centres – you need a degree or appropriate professional training. For many posts, academic qualifications are less important than personality – all are likely to emphasise attitude, approach and relevant experience. Resilience and diplomacy are particularly important qualities.

Community workers have to deal with all sorts of people: groups or individuals, members of the community and people in authority. There may be conflict between groups which the Community worker can help to reconcile. Often, problems can only be solved with persistence and/or compromise.

As far as formal training is concerned, youth and community courses, and some courses offering social work training, can be particularly relevant. There are also a few degree courses at honours level covering community studies, youth studies, urban studies, etc. Some degrees include options in community studies as part of courses in social studies, education, etc. Most courses require you to have two A levels, though mature students may be exempted. Youth and community work college courses normally require five GCSEs at grade C.

It is important to have relevant experience – whether voluntary or paid – in areas such as counselling and advisory work, social work, youth work and local politics.

Some typical job advertisements

Assistant Community Relations Officer – *Do you have the skill, experience and commitment needed to promote racial equality and eliminate discrimination? The Officer will undertake a wide range of duties such as Education, Youth and Project Work. The applicant should have experience of working with ethnic minority groups.*

Community Play Organiser – *A committed, experienced and enthusiastic professional is required by the Borough Recreation Department to promote children's play in the seven permanent play centres and the mobile holiday caravans. Preference will be given to candidates with appropriate qualifications and experience.*

Assistant Nurseries Organiser – *to assist in the running of the Committee for Community Relations' five nurseries and one playgroup, including development of existing anti-racist work demonstrating good practice in multi-racial nurseries. Background and good experience of under-fives work required, as well as experience of working with Afro-Caribbean, Asian and other ethnic minority communities.*

Detached Youth & Community Worker – Ethnic Minorities – *Applications are invited from suitably qualified and experienced people for the above newly-created post, to work in predominantly Asian communities. Candidates should be knowledgeable in all aspects of racial disadvantage, have strong organising ability and the expertise to become involved in the community, identify needs and devise strategies to encourage self-help and greater awareness of resources available.*

CHARITY & RELIGIOUS WORK

W hilst by far the largest part of charity work is done by unpaid helpers, charities and voluntary organisations themselves employ many people in both part-time and full-time work. These people may help those in need by raising and administering funds, doing research work, encouraging others to help themselves, or may work as advisers or carers. There are salaried positions for mature adults who have gained paid or voluntary experience.

Some salaries and wages paid by voluntary organisations are low. However, the larger organisations now offer good pay to attract more highly skilled people, who can cut costs in other ways and raise funds more effectively. Jobs are mostly the same as those found in the public or commercial sectors, in the areas of publicity, advertising and fundraising, financial control, retailing (a number of charities run chains of shops), and management. Large organisations are often looking for people who have a proven track record in the voluntary work sector, or who have transferable skills from another sector.

Types of voluntary organisations

Voluntary organisations can be divided into four categories:

■ **Those providing services directly to people in need** – e.g. Barnardo's, Help the Aged, NSPCC, Cyrenians. This is where the majority of the paid work is found – most commonly for social and care workers, nurses, paramedics, teachers, advice workers, managers and administrators, clerical and

secretarial staff, fund-raisers, public relations officers and information workers.

- **Those whose main function is research and publicity** – e.g. Child Poverty Action Group, Liberty, the various organisations researching into specific diseases. There are opportunities for researchers, administrators, clerical staff, public relations personnel, etc.

- **Those who mainly encourage self-help and community action** – e.g. Pre-school Learning Alliance, Mind, National Schizophrenia Fellowship. These mainly employ administrators, but some community workers too.

- **Those which aim to increase the effectiveness of voluntary bodies** – e.g. National Council for Voluntary Organisations, National Association of Citizens' Advice Bureaux, The Volunteer Centre UK. Again, these associations have administrative, information and publicity posts.

Vacancies can be found in the Wednesday edition of the *Guardian*, and also in weekly journals such as *New Statesman and Society, Community Care, Social Work Today*. These advertisements will give you some idea of the sort of work available, salaries, etc. A wide range of posts and higher-level jobs are offered through Charity Recruitment and Charity Appointments, respectively. See the Further Information section for details.

Religious work

Entrants to religious work of whatever denomination may be part of a group or team ministry, working within a local community and ministering to the needs of local people, with each member of the team contributing their own particular gifts to the work, or they may work on their own.

Other opportunities exist in specialisms such as chaplaincies to hospitals, prisons, universities and schools, to industry and to the Forces. Christian churches overseas also welcome men and women for missionary work. They need not only ordained clergy, but also lay Christians who are able to offer a wide variety of skills, and teachers, medical workers, agriculturalists, youth workers, accountants and many other professionally trained people are welcomed.

For further information, see *Care & Community* in the *Just the Job!* series.

just
THE
JOB

TEACHING IN NURSERY, INFANT & PRIMARY SCHOOLS

Teaching young children is a very responsible and important job. The teacher gives the children ideas about school and learning which will remain with them for the rest of their school career and, possibly, for life. It is demanding work, which can be very tiring, but can also be extremely rewarding. Young children constantly ask questions, show you what they have done and need your help, praise and encouragement. There are various age ranges in which you can specialise when training, e.g. three to seven, five to eleven, eight to thirteen. Virtually all new entrants to teaching are graduates.

Learning through doing

In teaching the youngest children, the emphasis is very much on learning through playing, experiencing and doing. The teacher is as much concerned with developing children's language abilities and social skills, as with more formal things like the beginnings of reading, writing, arithmetic, science and other subjects in the national curriculum.

Older primary children, who have gained the skills and concentration to do more sustained work, may require a somewhat different approach. In all cases, the teacher aims to provide challenges and experiences to develop and expand the child's curiosity and knowledge.

Planning, flexibility and sometimes being mum or dad

Good teachers organise their day carefully, planning what they want particular children to practise or experience. The children in a class spend a lot of the time working in small groups, or individually, on different activities, so teachers must be very well organised.

Yet teachers of young children can't be inflexible, or they would miss opportunities for learning. If workers dig a hole in the road outside the classroom, the teacher is wiser to let the children learn about roads and noise, than to try to ignore it! The day is more flexible than in a secondary school – bells don't ring every 45 minutes.

Generally, teachers of young children make a lot of their own teaching materials. All this has to be fitted in with assessment, and evaluation of each child's progress.

With nursery-age children and infants, the teacher often has to be a substitute parent, helping them with shoelaces, tending minor ills and sorting out their problems. Nursery schools and some infant schools have **nursery nurses** to help, but they are rather rare in infant/primary schools. Here **education support** or **teaching assistants** may help to look after the children (see section on non-teaching jobs in schools, below). Working with three-year-olds in a nursery school will involve assisting with very basic aspects of the children's development – including speech and physical coordination.

The teacher in a nursery, infant or primary school usually spends most of his or her time with the same group of children. This means a good relationship can be built up, but it also produces its own stresses, because small children are very demanding. In some schools, two teachers may share responsibility for a larger group of children, to allow for flexibility in activities. Classrooms may be 'open-plan', with furniture and carpeting separating areas for different types of work.

There may be specialists for some 'subjects', such as physical education, music, mathematics, etc.

Schools

Schools vary enormously in size, from those with less than thirty children in some villages, to city schools with over 600. The size of the school affects the day-to-day job. In a small school of around 60 children, there would typically be three teachers and small, mixed-age classes – one for infants up to about seven, one for lower juniors up to nine, and one for top juniors up to eleven. By comparison, a larger school may have one or two teachers for each year and classes of over 30 children.

In bigger schools, there are more opportunities for teachers to take on special responsibility for areas such as language, mathematics or music, and the higher paid 'special responsibility' posts.

What it takes

Teachers of young children need a wide range of abilities, interests and skills. Some of these attributes may be developed during training; others may already be held.

- Music, art and craft skills are always welcome.
- Interests like physical education and drama are also valued.
- Sound health is important. The job is physically demanding and teachers are exposed to all sorts of coughs and colds in schools. A teacher who is frequently off sick is a liability!

However, do note that some disabled people have successfully made careers in teaching; if you are disabled, you will need to make careful enquiries before applying for a training course.

QUALIFYING AS A TEACHER

Teaching is now an all-graduate profession, so you must have a degree. The main route into primary level teaching is through

the Bachelor of Education (BEd) degree. There are a few Postgraduate Certificate in Education (PGCE) courses which train would-be primary teachers, but competition for places is fierce. On a BEd course, you will study a primary level national curriculum subject to degree level as well as train to teach across all subjects of the primary curriculum. For the PGCE route, your previous education should provide the *'necessary foundation for work as a primary school teacher'*. Institutions will advise on their own specific entry requirements.

A national curriculum for teacher training was introduced in September 1997. Students have to reach defined standards in subject knowledge and basic classroom skills.

School/college-leavers

To be accepted on a degree course, you usually require:

■ a minimum of two A levels or the equivalent (likely to be three grade Cs for BEds in the future);

- supporting GCSEs which must include English and maths (grades A-C);
- for students born on or after 1 September 1979, a GCSE in a science subject at grade A-C is required for entry to primary teacher training from September 1998.

Advanced GNVQs are suitable for entry to higher education. However, evidence of the content of the course being relevant to the school curriculum is required. GNVQ students may therefore be asked for an additional A level in a primary curriculum subject.

Adults

The degree course entry requirements mentioned above may be relaxed for some mature entrants, whose applications are considered on individual merit. Over-21s with few or no qualifications wanting to train for teaching could consider following an Access course. These courses are offered at many further education colleges and are designed as an alternative to GCSEs and A levels for entry to degree and other higher education courses (minimum age varies between 21 and 24 years).

You usually need to state a particular subject specialism when you apply to train for primary teaching. Admissions tutors will look for subject relevance in the A levels or the Access course content.

Note: All applicants to teacher training are expected to have GCSEs at grade C or above in both English language and maths (or equivalent qualifications). Some colleges will allow applicants over 25 to take an entrance test in lieu of a qualification in English and/or maths, if they have had no opportunity to gain exam passes.

There are **employment-based training** schemes for graduates and for people with at least two years' successful experience of higher education. The Teacher Training Agency (TTA) can advise you.

See also the next section, on teaching in secondary schools, for more information about training to teach.

Independent training

There are also the independent education training systems, most of which follow a particular, sometimes individual, philosophical approach to the education of very young children. For example, there are the Rudolf Steiner schools which train their own staff to encourage child development and learning in line with Steiner's beliefs. Montessori training establishments are based on Dr Montessori's ideas of freedom for the child to learn in a carefully planned environment. Training to teach by one of these systems is unacceptable on its own for the state school system, and leads rather to jobs in privately-run nurseries, nursery and junior schools. These courses are shorter than normal teaching courses (one or two academic years), and some Montessori training centres offer part-time and distance-learning courses.

PROSPECTS

Full-time and part-time jobs are reasonably easy to find, and there is concern over a growing shortage of primary teachers in the next decade. Many primary schools now accept four-year-olds into mainstream education. This will inevitably lead to more recruitment of teachers of the very young. In the primary sector, church-controlled schools are common and they may require staff (especially headteachers) to be practising members of the appropriate religion.

TEACHING IN SECONDARY SCHOOLS

Unlike teachers in primary schools, secondary teachers are usually specialists in particular subjects. Most new entrants have taken a degree in their subject of interest, followed by a postgraduate teaching qualification, or they have specialised in the subject during their Bachelor of Education (BEd) degree course.

The subjects that you can train to teach are largely dictated by the national curriculum and by the A levels that you take. Job opportunities in teaching will depend on the subjects you can offer an employer. In general, the subject areas with the greatest shortage of suitable applicants are mathematics, physics, chemistry, business studies, music, modern languages, religious education, information technology and design technology. However, shortages of teachers in nearly every secondary school subject have been predicted over the next few years.

There are also various specialisations into which experienced teachers can move after some in-service training to gain additional expertise or qualifications. For instance, the majority of schools offer pupils a programme of social and personal education, including careers education. Another area is remedial teaching of pupils with special needs. Schools are organised into forms or tutor groups and most teachers have a tutorial role in addition to their teaching commitment.

There are opportunities for promotion to the responsibilities of head of year groups, head of lower or upper school, deputy or headteacher. These posts may entail responsibilities for:

- discipline in the school;
- curriculum planning;
- liaison with primary schools and local industry;
- timetabling and general administration.

Increments are paid to teachers for extra pastoral or management responsibilities. Teachers do get recognition of their contribution to a school over a period of time, even if they have had no increase in responsibility, because of the extended basic teaching pay scale.

Drama teaching

Drama teachers can work in both state-maintained and independent schools where drama is part of the curriculum. Many teachers of drama also offer another teaching subject, often English. There are opportunities in colleges of further education, universities and other higher education institutions, specialist drama schools, theatre groups, youth theatre workshops and arts centres.

For information about working in the performing arts, see the section on drama, acting & dance, below.

TRAINING TO TEACH

Teachers in state schools undergo approved teacher training leading to Qualified Teacher Status (QTS). Independent schools may employ teachers without QTS, but increasingly expect it. Usually you train to teach pupils within a specific age range – nursery, infant, infant/junior, junior, junior/secondary, middle school and secondary. In England and Wales, once you are qualified you are eligible to teach any age range, despite being trained for a limited age-group only – though a complete change would be difficult and unusual. In Scotland, it is necessary to be qualified specifically for the age range you teach.

A national curriculum for teacher training in primary schools was introduced in September 1997, and for secondary teacher training in 1998. Check with the Teacher Training Agency (TTA) for up-to-date details.

From September 1998, students on courses in science, maths, design and technology, modern foreign languages, religious education and music may be eligible for funding through the **Secondary Subject Shortage Scheme**. Awards are made by individual teacher training institutions and you should contact these for more information.

Entry qualifications

Teaching in state schools is now, for new entrants, generally an all-graduate profession. Your degree could be a BEd (Bachelor of Education), a BA or BSc (Hons) with Qualified Teacher Status, or a degree in some other subject together with a postgraduate teaching qualification (PGCE). The only possible exceptions to this are employment-based training schemes mentioned below.

School/college-leavers: To get on to a degree course normally requires a minimum of two A levels or the equivalent, and supporting GCSEs, which must include English and maths (grades A–C). Very rarely, potential PE, dance, drama and music teachers may be accepted for training with one A level, if they offer an extremely high standard in their practical subject.

Advanced GNVQs are suitable for entry to Higher Education. However, evidence of the content of the course being relevant to the school curriculum is required. GNVQ students may therefore be asked for an additional A level in a national curriculum subject.

Adults: Degree course entry requirements may be relaxed for some mature entrants. Adults with few or no qualifications wanting to train for teaching could consider following an Access Course (minimum age varies between 21 and 24 years). There are also some taster courses, and special courses for people returning to teaching after a break. The TTA can advise you.

The first degree route
The BEd, or sometimes BSc or BA honours degree with QTS, are combined degree and professional teacher training courses, which let you pursue academic study of one or more subjects, whilst also studying the theory and practice of teaching. You can take such degrees at colleges of higher education and at universities. Most courses run for four years, although there is now an increasing number of three-year degree courses. You can train for any age range, but this route tends to be regarded as most suitable for nursery, junior and the lower years of secondary rather than for sixth form and other exam-oriented teaching. Secondary BEds are available mainly in business studies, craft, design technology, home economics, mathematics, physical education, physical sciences and religious education. If you change your mind about teaching, your degree will still allow you entry into many other careers.

The postgraduate route
You can follow a first degree with a one-year teacher training course leading to a Postgraduate Certificate in Education (PGCE). There are also a few two-year PGCE courses which offer subject conversion as well as teacher training, and some part-time courses. The Open University, now the biggest provider of PGCE courses in the country, offers a part-time distance learning PGCE which takes eighteen months. Students can specialise in primary teaching, or in a particular secondary subject.

Your degree normally needs to be in a subject taught in schools, or to have included a large amount of subject matter relevant to curricular work – for instance, English, geography, languages, mathematics, sciences. Degrees in subjects like law or town planning are not recommended. Subjects like engineering or biochemistry might be acceptable, however, since large amounts of basic mathematics or science would have been covered in the course. Check with individual institutions.

The postgraduate route is generally thought to be the most suitable for those who wish to teach academic subjects to examination level in secondary education. It also keeps open other career options. There is keen competition for places on postgraduate courses for applicants with degrees in subjects such as history and social sciences. However, the government wants to promote recruitment to 'shortage' subjects (see above).

Other routes into teaching
Special two-year shortened BEd courses
If you wish to enter initial teacher training and have satisfactorily completed the equivalent of one or two years of higher education, you can follow a two-year shortened BEd course. These courses suit mature people with DipHEs, HNDs, professional or technical qualifications and experience, wishing to train to teach subjects such as maths, physics, chemistry, balanced science, technology, modern languages, Welsh and design technology.

Employment-based training routes
In England and Wales, the **Graduate Teacher Programme** is designed for those who have a degree and want to combine employment in a school with training that leads to Qualified Teacher Status. The **Registered Teacher Programme** runs along similar lines and is open to those with two years' higher education (e.g HND or DipHE). These programmes usually last one to two years: further information is available from the TTA.

School-centred initial teacher training courses (SCITT)
These are available in a limited number of school consortia and City Technology Colleges. They aim to encourage postgraduate entry to teaching of those whose first degree is relevant to the

school curriculum, and lead to QTS. Details from the Graduate Teacher Training Registry.

PROSPECTS

For experienced and qualified teachers there are opportunities for promotion up to the level of **deputy** or **headteacher**. Increments are paid to other teachers for extra pastoral or management responsibilities. In-service training is available to gain additional expertise or qualifications. There are limited opportunities as **advisers** and **inspectors** of schools, and **lecturers** on teacher training courses.

Other opportunities

Other possibilities for qualified teachers include teaching abroad; working as an education officer for a museum, a field centre or a charity; working on a special research project; publishing, etc.

Some teachers prefer educational positions where they do not have long-term responsibility for their students. Occasionally positions arise which would suit trained educationists who have specific research interests, to work with particular institutions or organisations, teaching aspects of their subject to groups of visitors or short-term residents. These educationists talk to many children and young people during the course of a working week, whilst researching, advising on, or writing background notes for, displays, handouts, quizzes and questionnaires for use by visitors to the particular centre. This might be a bird reserve, an ecology field station or a museum, displaying collections of anything, from musical instruments to fossils. Such teachers may be employed by the Civil Service, local education authorities, or other bodies such as the Wildlife Trust, RSPB, etc.

TEACHING SPORT & PE

Teachers of physical education work mostly in secondary schools, teaching games, gymnastics, dance, athletics, swimming and, perhaps, outdoor activities, such as canoeing and rock climbing. They also organise matches and help with extracurricular clubs. Teaching is virtually an all-graduate profession for new entrants.

Physical education in schools is concerned both with encouraging pupils' skills and body management and with young people's healthy growth and development. It is also a useful preparation for the management of leisure time in later life.

PE specialists usually teach another subject – this could be any one of the curriculum options, but it is useful to offer a mainstream subject, such as English or mathematics. They may also be responsible for pupils studying PE up to GCSE and A level standard.

What it takes

PE teachers need:

- to want to help young people develop;
- a friendly but firm manner;
- patience;
- energy and fitness;
- organising skills;
- skill in sport and movement;
- a willingness to spend time in out-of-school and weekend activities.

Both state and independent schools can place a very high emphasis on PE, sport and team games, and specialist posts are frequently advertised. Managing teams is an important part of the work. Whilst there is no legal requirement for teachers in independent schools to have had formal teacher training (as there is in state schools), many independent schools insist on teachers being qualified and capable of teaching an additional subject.

TRAINING TO TEACH

See the section on training to teach in secondary schools.

Specialist training for graduates wishing to teach PE is available in a number of universities and colleges. Some of these courses may be taken after any degree, although some institutions prefer students who have taken PE, sports science or human movement as at least a major part of their undergraduate course. There is also evidence that employment prospects are better for students who have taken one of these subjects as their first degree. A limited number of one-year postgraduate courses are provided through school-centred initial teacher training courses.

For PE teaching, clearly a high level of physical fitness is demanded, and adult applicants need to be aware that their career opportunities could be very limited.

PROSPECTS

On the whole, people with a relevant degree plus a PGCE qualification from a university seem to have least difficulty in finding employment. Being able to offer a second teaching subject that is in demand will improve chances of getting a job. You should also think ahead to when you are older – as the physical aspects of the job become less attractive and more arduous, an alternative teaching subject will almost certainly be required. The areas where there is most demand for teachers at present are in the 'shortage' subjects of sciences, mathematics, modern languages and design technology.

Other openings

Sports coaching at sport and leisure centres does not demand such high academic qualifications, but you will be expected to have appropriate practical qualifications in your chosen sport or sports. See also the sections on outdoor pursuits and leisure and recreation management.

TEACHING DANCE

For those with a love of, and a special aptitude for, dance there are two main career prospects – performing and teaching. There are several options for performers, but, for all of them, you need to be very talented. To teach dance, you need a degree or a professional qualification.

A range of opportunities exists, both as a private teacher and in independent and state schools. Dance teachers work with people of all ages and both sexes – from three-year-olds who are learning ballet, tap, etc, up to adults wishing to learn ballroom dancing, modern dance, or dance as a means of exercise. All teachers of dance should be good communicators and enjoy teaching, if they are to be successful. Teaching is not just a second best for those who fail to make the grade as performers.

For private teaching, a high standard of personal performance and good appropriate qualifications, such as teacher training at a vocational school or professional qualifications from one of the teaching societies, are necessary, combined with a good business sense and capital if you want to run your own school. For teaching in state schools, a full teacher training is necessary, with the emphasis not so much on performing, as on dance as education and movement studies. To start training, you must normally have two A levels/Advanced GNVQ, plus supporting GCSEs at grade C, including English and maths.

DANCE COURSES IN FURTHER AND HIGHER EDUCATION

Some colleges of higher education and universities offer degrees in dance e.g. the universities of Middlesex, Brighton, Birmingham, Leicester De Montfort, and Surrey, Bretton Hall College and Roehampton Institute. As well as practical dance, these courses have an academic content, including such things as the physiology of movement and sociology of dance. In the main, these are not intended as courses for professional performers, but rather as general education or for intending teachers. Dance is also offered as one subject on a number of combined studies degree courses. Course information can be found in *University and College Entrance* and *The Compendium of Higher Education*, which should be in school and college careers libraries, careers service and public libraries. Many universities and colleges offer degrees and BTEC Higher National Diplomas in Performing Arts, which include dance.

Degrees in dance, as well as three-year vocational training courses, are also offered at London Contemporary Dance School, the College of the Royal Academy of Dancing, and the Laban Centre. These courses are much more practically-based, and many graduates would go on to careers as performers and dance teachers.

Some schools and colleges are piloting GNVQs in Performing Arts and the Entertainment Industries, and these should be more widely available from September 1998. There is a BTEC National Diploma in Performing Arts offered by a number of further education colleges.

Other opportunities with dance

Performance – see section on Drama, acting & dance, below.

Choreography involves creating new dances. It can be studied as an option on many vocational training courses. Consult the prospectuses of the various institutes for further information.

Notation, the recording of dance movements, involves using symbols to represent the detailed position of the body at any one moment. It is used mostly for recording and rehearsal purposes. There are two main systems – Benesh Movement Notation and Labanotation.

Dance therapy involves the use of movement and dance as a medium through which people with physical, mental and emotional difficulties can express themselves and develop.

TEACHING MUSIC

The educational world offers more opportunities for musicians than any other occupational field. Anybody can set up as a private music teacher, but the most reputable have very good qualifications, and are listed in the Incorporated Society of Musicians' Register of Professional Private Music Teachers. Class teachers in schools must be trained and qualified to teach. For graduates, this means taking a postgraduate certificate in education course, lasting one year, in order to obtain Qualified Teacher Status.

Musicians work in primary, middle, secondary and special schools; in colleges of music, colleges of further and higher education and universities; in music centres; and as private music teachers. Teachers of musical instruments can be appointed as peripatetic staff, and usually visit pupils in several schools.

Successful private teachers can earn a comfortable living, but many find that much of their work is done at weekends and in the evenings, i.e. outside normal school and working hours.

Other opportunities with music
There are one-year postgraduate courses in **music therapy**, which is concerned with the treatment, education and rehabilitation through music of adults and children with physical, mental or emotional difficulties. Posts are available with local education authorities, social services departments and hospitals.

You have to be exceptionally talented to make a career as a **performer** in any field. Most performers are drawn from

students from the colleges of music. Students who have studied for a music degree usually take a postgraduate course at one of the music colleges, in order to concentrate on perfecting their instrumental technique and expanding their repertoire, since, on the whole, university courses do not have a strong performance bias. Most trainee musicians seek every opportunity to perform, and this is often for young audiences and, often, in youth orchestras.

If you want a performing career as a pop artist or dance band musician, you need to be talented, and a proficient instrumentalist or singer if you're going to get anywhere. Although a college training is not essential, there are some degree and BTEC HND courses available in popular music. The City of Leeds College of Music offers a degree course in jazz studies.

For more opportunities in the field of music, see *Leisure, Sport & Entertainment* in the *Just the Job!* series.

NON-TEACHING JOBS IN SCHOOLS

All schools, whether in the private or state sector, have some non-teaching staff who have a variable degree of involvement with the children. The number and range of posts vary from school to school. For instance, a large comprehensive school has administrative, welfare, laboratory and library staff, while an infant school secretary will be a 'jack of all trades', doing secretarial and administrative work, and dealing with minor first aid.

Schools are responsible for their own budgets and administration, and have to provide lots of statistics for the annual 'league tables'. There is also paperwork associated with the national curriculum. Many schools choose to employ more non-teaching staff in order to free teachers from some of this extra administrative and technical work.

Because many of the non-teaching jobs in schools are only part-time, fit in with the school day and have school holidays, they are often attractive to working parents. Positions in school offices, for example, may be quite difficult to get because of their popularity. Schools are normally responsible for recruiting their own staff and usually advertise in the local press if they have a vacancy. There are also a lot of non-educational staff employed in further education colleges. While these jobs may be full-time or part-time, they are less likely to offer college holidays.

Administrative staff

There is a huge amount of paperwork and general administration to do in any school or college, so staff are needed at all levels – from basic clerical assistants to managers. At a basic level, work in a school office includes many tasks that you will find in any office, but also some which are particular to education. Duties can include:

- keeping school records – probably on computer;
- wordprocessing documents – from lesson timetables to parents' letters;
- photocopying and filing;
- dealing with orders and invoices;
- taking room bookings;
- dealing with examination entries;
- sorting the incoming and outgoing post;
- acting as receptionist to visitors to the school;
- taking telephone calls, messages and dealing with general enquiries.

In a small school, such as an infant or small primary school, one person is likely to be employed to undertake the range of office activities. The **school secretary**, as the position is often called, often becomes a friend to the children and, besides the duties already listed, deals with grazed knees, nosebleeds and other minor ills and troubles.

In a college or large school, (especially if the school is totally responsible for its own finances), you will find a number of administrative staff, each having different responsibilities. For example, some staff work as personal secretaries to people like the school or college principal; some work on the financial side; others concentrate on keeping computer records or on reception duties. Positions which include office management exist in some institutions.

The qualifications required for administrative work in a school vary from post to post. For a basic clerical position, you would be likely to need a minimum of two GCSEs at grade C; an administrative officer may require five GCSEs at grade C, including English and maths, and perhaps A levels or the equivalent. An older person with some experience may not need any academic qualifications. Wordprocessing skills and experience in other aspects of office work may be required for some posts. Office staff are also likely to have contact with parents and a wide range of other professional staff, so good communication skills – and, at times, tact and diplomacy – are useful!

Bursar

Many large schools, and particularly independent schools, employ a bursar. The bursar's particular responsibility is to manage the school's finances. This means keeping track of how the school budget is being spent, and ensuring the necessary financial records are kept correctly. Bursars also take responsibility for many aspects of the general business management of the school. He or she needs to work closely with the headteacher and other senior teaching staff in the school. Responsibilities can be wide and may include:

- managing administrative and other non-teaching staff;
- overseeing the maintenance of buildings;
- dealing with the administration of staff pay and recruitment;
- taking responsibility for contracts such as cleaning and school transport;
- ensuring the school is properly insured;
- in independent schools, the setting and collecting of fees.

Individual schools decide their own requirements in terms of experience and qualifications needed for bursars' posts. However, a background in accountancy or financial management is relevant, and would usually be essential.

Library/learning resources staff

Libraries in schools today contain far more than just books! You are likely to find computers, videos, cassettes and a variety of self-study materials, for example, which students can use in the library for studying on their own. Staff who work in the library have responsibility for all these learning materials, as well as the books, so are often called *learning resources* staff. Besides looking after books and other learning materials, librarians have a lot of contact with pupils and students, often teaching them to use the library's facilities. They may also be responsible for buying books and other resources.

While professional librarian qualifications are not always required, applicants holding qualifications, or with relevant experience, will generally have an advantage. As a minimum, staff would usually be expected to have five GCSEs at grade C or equivalent, including English. Colleges usually employ professionally-qualified librarians (see next section).

Education support assistants/teaching assistants

Support assistants work in primary, secondary and special schools doing various jobs in order to give teachers more time to teach. Jobs for general support assistants might include preparing displays and setting out apparatus, helping children change for games or PE, and supervising in the playground, dining hall and cloakrooms. Education support assistants' work is particularly important in special schools for children with physical disabilities or emotional difficulties, where caring for the children is very demanding. There are also jobs for support assistants in mainstream schools to help children with special needs to integrate and cope with the demands of an ordinary school day. This is a growing area, as more children with disabilities are educated in ordinary schools. In this case, the support assistant usually works with one child with special needs, rather than being a general help to the teacher. Such jobs are often part-time.

Several colleges are now running one-year part-time courses for **specialist teaching assistants** (STAs). STAs help teachers in primary schools with reading, writing and maths. Course applicants should have GCSE grade C in English and maths (or equivalent), or they may be accepted after interview or a test. Courses may have other entry conditions, such as being open only to assistants working in that local education authority.

Escort on school transport

Escorts are employed to look after some children travelling daily to and from special schools. These children usually have fairly severe physical disabilities, or behavioural difficulties. The escorts are responsible for the children from the time they leave their home until they are handed over to the school, and from school to home. They have to be very careful to know of alternative places to take the child if, for any reason, the parent is not there to look after them. This is a part-time job only.

School nurse

School nursing is part of the community nursing service. Nurses regularly spend time in schools, working closely with teachers, parents, doctors and other health professionals. They concentrate on checking the health of the pupils, are involved in immunisation programmes, and in assessments of individual children. Health education is the other very important part of the nurse's role. School nurse training courses are offered in a number of nurse training institutions, for qualified nurses.

Matron and assistant matron

These are usually boarding school jobs. Matrons act as house-keepers and substitute parents to children away at boarding school. They are responsible for such things as bedding, laundry, hygiene, and the health of the children. The matron will usually have one or more assistant matrons and will supervise the work of domestic cleaning staff. A matron could have a background in nursing or as a nursery nurse, or just the experience of having brought up a family. The main requirements are good organising ability, a friendly, approachable personality and patience. Assistant matrons are often drawn from students who have taken some kind of residential care course at a further education college.

Midday supervisory assistant

Midday supervisory assistants look after pupils during the lunch break at school. They supervise the dining room and, with young children, may cut up food or encourage children to eat their meals. They do not serve meals, lay tables or wash up. They supervise the pupils in the playground or inside during wet weather. Hours are normally very limited.

School meals service

The kitchen staff are generally part-timers and work on preparing, serving and washing up after school lunches. Many school kitchens now just heat and serve meals that have been cooked and chilled elsewhere. These jobs usually appeal to people with young families, for whom the hours of work are ideal.

Supervisors are likely to have experience of mass catering, and may need to be able to make a little money go a long way.

There is a great deal of difference between the supervisor's job in a small primary school and in an enormous comprehensive school. The supervisor in a large school will not only need to be an experienced caterer but also to be capable of organising quite a large staff. The school meals staff may be employed by a catering contractor rather than directly by the school.

Laboratory assistant/technician

Technicians look after the equipment and materials for the science departments of secondary schools; they may also be employed in colleges, within the science, engineering, technology or construction departments. In schools, technicians set up experiments for teachers and clear up after practical sessions. They have to make sure that stocks of chemicals are kept up, that equipment is in working order and there is enough of it. They have to work very closely with the science staff of the school. Some qualifications, especially in science subjects, would be required, at least to GCSE at grade C and commonly to A level or equivalent.

IT coordinator/computer technician

IT technicians provide computer expertise for both teachers and pupils in larger secondary schools. They have the responsibility for making sure systems are 'up and running' throughout the school and for carrying out any necessary repairs and adjustments to equipment. Experience and a good understanding of the computing field would be necessary for this kind of work.

Audio-visual technician/resources technician

Audio-visual technicians look after all the technical sound, vision and printing or reprographic equipment in a school. The equipment used varies tremendously from school to school and could include items like closed-circuit television, back projectors, cassette recorders, photocopiers, film projectors, video-players and recorders and complicated printing equipment.

Audio-visual technicians come from varied backgrounds and, in fact, the colleges which run courses for AV technicians say it is often very difficult devising courses for a group with such mixed abilities. If you had some experience in areas of work like photography, electronics, TV and radio repair or printing, you might well have a suitable background. Most courses are part-time for those already working, but there are a few two-year full-time courses which lead to a BTEC National Diploma in Audio-Visual Design, and part-time City & Guilds qualifications in Audio-Visual Techniques. These could be useful qualifications for this and other types of work in the communications and media industry.

Grounds staff

Grounds staff are usually responsible for sports pitches and school gardens, and possibly for greenhouses and cold frames used for environmental studies or similar subject areas. There will probably be only one member of staff in each school and therefore an experienced person is required. Amenity horticulture or groundsmanship skills, perhaps with appropriate qualifications, would be useful.

Caretaker

School caretakers look after school buildings, may oversee the work of the cleaners, and take responsibility for the security of the building and such things as the heating and plumbing. Often a house on the school site goes with the job, as caretakers may have to be available in the evenings for school events and lettings, when they go round putting out lights, shutting windows and locking doors. This is a job for a mature person. It's not the sort of job for which you need any qualifications, but caretakers need to be practical and have plenty of common sense.

WORKING IN LIBRARIES & INFORMATION SERVICES

Library and information work involves working with books, computer databases and with all the other modern methods of storing information. There is more routine work for library assistants, all of whom can now work towards the nationally-recognised NVQs in information and library service work. Many librarians and library assistants work with children and young people, looking after school library collections or running the children's sections of larger libraries.

Two main types of staff work in libraries – the **chartered librarians** and information professionals, and **library assistants**. These people do quite different jobs (though in very small libraries there is more overlap). Library assistants normally see to the routine running of the library. Librarians and information specialists are highly qualified professionals.

Books are just one means of storing information so that it can be found again. In public libraries, cassettes, records, CDs, and videos are all part of the library stock. Increasingly, systems other than print are used for storing information. Computers, microfilm and viewdata systems are used in nearly every library. These applications of new technology mean that information can be stored much more economically and found more rapidly and efficiently.

Where library professionals work

Although, not long ago, at least half of all librarians worked in public libraries, they now account for only 28% of members of the Library Association. There is increasing employment for librarians in other sectors of business and industry, news broadcasting and journalism – wherever there are information needs. Besides public lending libraries, the main types of libraries where you would work with children and young people are:

■ careers centre libraries;
■ libraries in schools and colleges;
■ libraries in hospitals, prisons, etc.

School and college libraries are found in technical, agricultural, music and art colleges. Some schools may just offer library assistant or clerical assistant posts, but, in most areas, secondary school and college libraries are managed by fully-qualified professional staff.

What the work involves

The work of librarians (or information officers) and their assistants varies a lot, according to where they are employed.

They *select* books, periodicals, magazines, cassettes and other materials. They must balance the needs of their users against the available resources. In a public or general interest library, an awareness of local tastes, authors, subjects and publishers is essential to achieve greatest effect. In the public library service, library and information staff often choose books and other materials as a team, sharing their knowledge. In a special college or academic library, the users may influence decisions on which items are to be bought.

They *research* information to help users solve a particular problem. The librarian or information officer uses reference books, bibliographies, periodicals and magazines, computer databases or any other available source to provide the best possible answer to the person making the enquiry. This detective work can be a great source of job satisfaction, and forms a high proportion of the work in all types of libraries. In a public library, the enquiries can be very wide-ranging, and a librarian may assist children and young people with:

■ homework topics;
■ independent learning;
■ those doing quizzes and competitions;
■ information on foreign countries.

What it takes

Many librarians like books and enjoy reading, but this is not essential for the job. More important qualities are having a lively personality and constant intellectual curiosity.

Other important qualities include:

■ being able to deal with all kinds of people in a pleasant, tactful and efficient manner without getting flustered;
■ having a keen interest in searching out information, whatever the format, to satisfy enquirers in all types of libraries and information services – including retrieving information from computer databases;
■ being able to organise one's own work and that of the staff, to achieve efficiency;
■ having a wide general knowledge, some familiarity with foreign languages, an interest in current events and a reliable memory. A good visual memory is important for the librarian of an art collection;
■ being prepared to work shifts and, in most public and academic libraries, not minding having to work some evenings and some Saturdays, as these are the times most convenient to many users;
■ in most, but not necessarily all jobs, being reasonably fit – an important consideration in a job which may keep you on your feet;
■ a high degree of professionalism.

TRAINING

Professional library and information work is an all-graduate profession. There are two main ways of training and either route is acceptable for work in the public library service. For some special and academic library posts, the second option may be preferable.

A degree in library/information studies, taken singly or as a joint honours degree with another subject.

A degree in any subject followed by a full-time or part-time postgraduate course in library/information studies or information science. Bursaries and studentships for full-time postgraduate courses are very few and must be applied for through the academic institution offering the course. You should get some practical experience in a library or in an information-related job before a postgraduate course, particularly if applying for a bursary or studentship. Usually, nine months to a year's work experience is required; details of some temporary positions are available from the Library Association from October to July. Degree-level qualifications are required for admission to postgraduate courses.

ENTRY REQUIREMENTS

Minimum requirements for degree courses are usually two A levels/Advanced GNVQ/BTEC National Diploma, plus supporting GCSEs. You will need English language GCSE at grade C or an equivalent qualification; a foreign language and a science are useful.

There are information posts in some organisations which can be entered by graduates without professional qualifications, but your career would be limited if you were not fully qualified. Most library and information professionals belong to the Library Association, the chartered professional body in the UK. To satisfy the Library Association's criteria for admission to its professional Register of Chartered Members, most candidates will have successfully completed a degree or postgraduate course accredited by the Association, followed by a minimum of one year's approved training while in a first professional post, plus one or two years' experience prior to submitting their application. For detailed further information and a list of courses, write to the Library Association.

Library assistant

Library assistants help run libraries. Their job involves:

- issuing books and other materials to borrowers, often using a computer system;
- checking returned items and putting them back on the shelves;
- helping people to find books and information;
- sending reminders to borrowers who keep books and other materials too long;
- informing people that items they have requested have arrived;
- helping with filing and other administrative and clerical work;
- dealing with enquiries.

Library assistants can work in any type of library mentioned above, including mobile library vans. To be good at the work, you need to get on well with all sorts of people, and to be patient – not easily flustered by sudden rushes of work or difficult customers. A good memory helps, and a liking for dealing with information. 'Awkward' hours are usually entailed, with some evening/weekend work, but this is not always unpopular. There is often scope for part-time work.

GETTING STARTED

Educational requirements are usually a minimum of four GCSEs at grade C, with English being the most important subject. The basic duties are learned on-the-job, but you can also take a one-year, part-time or distance-learning City & Guilds Library and Information Assistants Certificate. A Higher National Certificate on Library and Information Science is available by distance learning over two years. National Vocational Qualifications in Information and Library Services at levels 2 to 4 are also available, but it is unlikely that NVQs will eliminate the need for a degree to achieve professional status.

Vacancies for library assistants can be found in local newspapers and, occasionally, the *Library Association Record* Vacancies Supplement, which is sent out only to members of the Association and mainly carries professional posts.

Promotion opportunities are rather limited, though there are posts for Senior Library Assistants in larger libraries. The Library Association produces an information booklet on job-hunting for members.

CAREERS IN OUTDOOR PURSUITS

The term *outdoor pursuits* includes a wide range of activities – such as climbing, orienteering, riding, sailing, windsurfing and canoeing, even parachuting and hanggliding. It also covers different types of employment within the fields of leisure and education. Qualifications in your chosen activity can be as important as academic qualifications for some jobs, while others may require a degree.

Teaching in schools

There are few opportunities for people to be employed in schools, whether state or private, specifically as teachers of outdoor pursuits. (See the *Handbook of Initial Teacher Training*, published by NATFHE, for details of all BEd and PGCE courses, which includes courses where physical education is the main subject specialism.)

Teachers with an interest in outward bound activities may well be able to find some opportunities for developing children's interest in outdoor pursuits, but this might be outside normal school work – for instance, through after-school clubs, the Duke of Edinburgh's Award Scheme or taking occasional parties of children to outdoor activity centres.

Teaching & instructing in outdoor activity centres

Local education authorities maintain outdoor activity/education centres, to which schools send parties of children for a few days or a week at a time. Privately-run outdoor pursuits centres may also cater for school groups, or for people of any age on activity holidays. Some centres cater for people sent through their work, as part of personal development or management training. Activities on offer can range greatly, and include rock climbing, hiking, orienteering and various water sports. Some centres specialise in a particular activity, such as sailing or skiing.

Outdoor pursuits centres require well-trained and experienced staff. Some would want qualified teachers, while others would accept instructors trained in individual activities such as canoeing or mountaineering. Outdoor pursuits centres are now regulated under the Adventure Activities Licensing Scheme, which ensures that facilities and staff conform to strict safety and training requirements. Therefore, having recognised qualifications is important. The work may be seasonal, but vacancies, when they occur, are very competitive.

Youth work

It is certainly an asset for youth workers and others involved in young people's leisure activities to be keen on outdoor pursuits. Full-time professional youth workers, and those who are youth leaders, Scouters, Guiders, etc, in their spare time, can use an interest in such activities. But it's only incidental to the work; organisational abilities and a genuine interest in young people are a much greater priority.

QUALIFICATIONS

Each activity, such as canoeing or horseriding, has its own controlling body which trains instructors. A useful initial qualification is the Central Council of Physical Recreation's Basic Expedition Training Award. National Vocational Qualifications have been developed for leaders, teachers and instructors working in outdoor education.

For this kind of work, besides being keen on outdoor pursuits, you need to enjoy working with people. Instructors need to be good at communicating with, motivating and leading people.

Other opportunities

- People with very high-level qualifications in a particular activity could become trainers.
- Experienced divers could become instructors at centres which train professional divers.
- Keen sailors can consider crewing for chartered and privately owned yachts, or on sail-training vessels.
- Suitably experienced and qualified people can train people to become coaches or instructors.
- Limited openings exist in the provision of activities for young people and adults with disabilities.
- Sport, outdoor activities and physical education play a very important part in training in the armed forces.

ENTERTAINING & SHOW BUSINESS

Entertainer describes a wide range of performers: comedians, cabaret singers, musicians, dancers, puppeteers, conjurors, mime artists, jugglers, acrobats, impressionists — even animal trainers. There are also host/hostess-entertainers, who organise and entertain young audiences in places like holiday centres, large hotels and on board cruise ships.

Where do entertainers work?

- Television offers opportunities for top-grade entertainers, but it's very hard to break in.
- Seaside resort theatres put on pantomimes and summer shows.
- Holiday camps/centres and theme parks offer opportunities for people to organise social events and entertain as well. This work is a training ground for many hopeful entertainers.
- Circuses employ certain specialist entertainers.
- Other opportunities include entertaining at events like children's parties and medieval banquets.
- Street entertainers can operate under licence from local authorities and police in shopping precincts or town centres, or as part of festivals and carnivals.

GETTING STARTED

Decide where your talents lie, and whether you really have the drive to make it in the entertainment business. Probably you will spend a long time as an amateur or part-time entertainer, doing evening and weekend performances, whilst having an ordinary daytime job, before you consider going professional.

However, at a fairly early stage, you are likely to need an agent to get bookings for you. You'll have to convince them that you have an act that people will want, and that you are 100% reliable. There are many agents in London and other city centres who book for clubs and events like conventions, conferences, dances and so forth.

Things to think about...

- Being an entertainer is an odd, stressful and chancy business. There are many people around in show business who, if not exactly dishonest, are quite prepared to make money out of the unwary and inexperienced.
- Nobody gets to the top without some knocks, and most never get to the top anyway. You'll need a lot of perseverance and some good luck.
- The lifestyle may be difficult. The hours are unsocial, as you are working when most people are at leisure. It can be stressful working in different places all the time, sometimes with hostile audiences.
- Regular work is unusual, so earnings can be very irregular too. You will certainly need an alternative way of making your living, if necessary.
- There may be opportunities to work abroad.

Working in circuses

Traditional circuses have been around for a long time, although changing public tastes have led to fewer animal acts. Most circus performers have been born into the business and, as a result, outsiders find it difficult to enter, even if they have the skills and talent.

A circus also needs a **manager** with one/two **assistant managers**, a **publicity and advertising assistant** and **box office**

staff. Jobs include planning circus venues, ordering fodder for the animals, making up salaries, buying food and other supplies, obtaining permission to display posters on hoardings, arranging for the printing of programmes and selling tickets. The smooth running of the performance relies on the **ring crew**, who set up the props and equipment, **electricians** and **spotlight operators**.

Travelling circuses sometimes find it difficult to recruit and keep skilled technical staff because most people prefer to work in a settled spot rather than to move continually. This means there are sometimes vacancies for mechanics, lighting technicians and electricians and, occasionally, even opportunities for training.

Instrumentalists and performers are not normally engaged locally. Acts are booked through a London agent who is in touch with performers all over the world. Other jobs can be found by approaching individual circuses.

Unlike the traditional tented circus, there is now a New Circus movement which uses traditional jugglers, acrobats and tightrope walkers, but no animals. New Circus is more related to performing arts than traditional circus; performances may take place in arts centres, pubs, clubs and in the street. A one-year foundation course in New Circus skills is available at 'Circomedia' in Bristol – 'the academy of circus arts and physical theatre' – as well as shorter courses and one-day workshops.

Puppetry

Puppetry – glove puppets, marionettes, object animation, etc – is a very specialised area of entertainment, but one which is becoming increasingly popular. Opportunities include:

- one-person shows working at children's parties;
- travelling two/three people shows;
- resident theatre companies;
- working in television and film;
- object animation – for television adverts, etc.

There is very little formal training. A degree course is available at the Central School in London, and other theatre studies/drama courses may have a puppetry element. There are several degree courses in animation. You may be able to attend short courses and evening classes to improve your skills. If you show talent, an existing puppet company may take you on as a trainee.

DRAMA, ACTING & DANCE

Careers in drama, acting and dance are competitive, demanding and often insecure, but many people think of them as something challenging and rewarding which they would love to do. Very few people become famous – but stardom is not everyone's goal. Many people enjoy performing with, and perform in front of, young people.

Professional acting

Actors must be dedicated and they need plenty of stamina. Acting is a particularly disciplined business. As well as memorising lines and movements, actors may have to change their accent, posture and appearance. Although young people can form a rapt and highly appreciative audience, they can also be quick to detect and criticise any sloppiness in performance. Come what may, the actors must be ready when the curtain goes up, and rehearsals must never be missed unless you are at death's door! The unreliable actor or actress is the one who doesn't get the job. A high degree of responsibility towards fellow performers and to the production is always essential.

Most actors will experience long periods of unemployment, long and unsocial hours, and poor levels of pay. All actors need to be prepared to face lots of rejections in their career.

GETTING STARTED

To act in theatre and television it is advisable to belong to Equity, the actor's union. Most employers have casting agreements with Equity. This means that they will engage only those performers who have previous professional experience, and who are usually members of the union, or an agreed quota of newcomers. This doesn't make work easy to get, but it does ensure that certain minimum standards of pay and conditions can be maintained and that a minimum standard of ability can be demanded.

If you want to act in films, television, radio, repertory theatre or in London's West End, the easiest way to get started is by the drama school route. Taking a course accredited by the National Council for Drama Training at a drama school means that you are registered with Equity. Students from unaccredited courses, and those without training, may find it much more difficult to break in. Other ways include becoming a chorus singer or a dancer, or getting into one of the small alternative fringe and children's theatre companies. However, working for a non-Equity company leaves you without protection and open to exploitation.

- **Television** offers opportunities for leading and supporting roles, walk-on and 'extra' parts, stunt work and commercials.
- Regional **repertory theatres**, small-scale touring companies and theatre-in-education companies provide another source of employment. This area of work makes large demands in terms of performance skills and dedication. Conditions 'on the road' can be rough, the pay poor and the work physically demanding. You may have to take several roles in two or even three performances a day, whilst learning new parts for the *next* production. Some companies offer fairly secure long-term contracts; others have insecure profit-sharing (or loss-sharing!) arrangements.
- There are **theatres** in major cities, including London's West End, which depend mainly on public or private subsidy. Economic pressures have affected the cast sizes and, therefore, job opportunities. Many young actors still start out in reper-

tory companies which offer short seasons of farces, thrillers, contemporary plays and classics.

- **Films** offer limited opportunities. The UK film industry has been through several lean years, but there are signs of an upward trend in the British Movie business.
- **Radio** drama still offers a lot of openings, at both national and regional level.
- Miscellaneous work includes **dubbing**, **voice-overs**, industrial **training videos**.

Other careers using drama

Drama is generally regarded as one of the performing arts, but there are many other opportunities besides performance in the theatre. These include production, stage management, administration, theatre-in-education, lighting, wardrobe, etc.

There is also the use of drama as therapy. **Drama therapists** use dramatic techniques to help patients – often children and adolescents – with mental and physical handicaps and illnesses. Through drama, patients can express aspects of their problems which they are unable to do in their day-to-day lives. Drama therapy is only a small profession and therapists may be employed on a part-time basis, having to work in several different places to get a full workload.

EDUCATION AND TRAINING

There are two main routes for drama training – attending a drama school or following a degree course at a college or university. Most courses are broad and include voice, mime and television technique. Entry requirements usually include A levels or a BTEC National Diploma in Performing Arts.

An Advanced GNVQ in Performing Arts and Entertainment Industries is being piloted in a few schools and colleges, and should be widely available from September 1998. This will be an equivalent qualification.

There are specialised courses in directing and stage management.

BTEC National Diplomas in Performing Arts
These are two-year courses, equivalent in standard to A levels, and normally requiring four GCSEs at grade C for entry. They are vocationally- and practically-based.

Drama schools
There are only a few drama schools in Britain and competition for places is intense. Normal entry varies between 17 and 25 years old. Exact requirements vary, but a good general education would be required with many students having two A levels or a BTEC National Diploma in Performing Arts. Selection depends on an entrance audition. The more experience you have before going to drama school, the better will be your chance of getting a place. Courses usually last between two and three years.

Degrees
Students who wish to take a degree (including drama/theatre studies, diploma in dramatic art, or a recognised course for teachers) must have the appropriate entry qualifications. These are normally five GCSEs at grade C with two subjects at A level

– other equivalents are often acceptable. To train as a teacher in state schools, you must also have GCSE at grade C in mathematics and English. Competition for places on degree courses that include drama is very high.

Graduates of drama courses may need further training in a drama school, before they can expect to start work. The Guildhall School of Music & Drama offers a performance-based degree course equivalent in status to drama school practical qualifications.

There are a few postgraduate courses in, for instance, writing plays, production, design and criticism. Two or three drama schools offer courses for the teaching of drama, in conjunction with colleges of higher education.

Awards
If you are trying to be assessed for a discretionary award to study drama, remember that you can only apply to attend a drama school which is recognised by the Department for Education and Employment. You may be required to attend an interview with your local authority. Today, however, it is extremely difficult to gain such an award. The majority of students have to pay their way through training.

Dance
Like all the performing arts, dancing is an overcrowded profession. Dancers have an additional problem not shared by actors or musicians: even if they are successful, their career is short. In any type of dance, few dancers go on beyond the age of 35. Many don't even work to that age, if a serious or recurring injury forces them to stop. They have to be fit, well-trained and look right. There are limited opportunities for a six-foot ballerina or a five-foot premier male dancer! Modern dance has less rigid requirements concerning height, but appearance and physique can, nevertheless, play an important role. Amongst those dancers who do not make the grade to performance artist,

many pursue their interest through a rewarding career teaching dance to younger would-be ballerinas and modern dancers.

For a performance career, most training is provided by the independent dance schools. A list of accredited courses can be obtained from the Council for Dance Education and Training. Competition for places is fierce, and discretionary awards are very difficult to obtain: contact dance colleges and your local education authority awards department for information.

Classical ballet

Ballet dancers start very young. Unless you have already begun serious training by the age of sixteen, you are unlikely to succeed. Full-time vocational courses (2–3 years) usually start at 16, after which a student would audition for ballet companies. The Royal Ballet School has a particular function in providing dancers for the Royal Ballet companies. Other schools, including the Central School of Ballet, offer training for wider careers opportunities. A very few dancers move on to choreography.

Contemporary and theatre dance

This includes all sorts of stagework, from experimental modern dance to musicals and the chorus line in pantomime, working in clubs, on cruise ships and in pop videos. Television offers a limited range of work for experienced dancers who have generally had an apprenticeship in stagework. Training is important, but does not require such an early start as with ballet. You can even start in your early twenties, especially if you are male. Contemporary and theatre dancers have often had ballet training at some stage. Students of established dance schools are the ones most likely to find work. Dancers, like actors, must have an Equity card to work in mainstream professional theatre, film and television. Equity is the performers' union and controls entry to these areas of work. Trained dancers may find it easier to get work than actors.

Ballroom dancing

The way into ballroom dancing as a professional is via amateur competitions. A few dancers can make a professional career, but usually only for a limited period. Teaching is the main source of work. Other areas of employment within the field of ballroom dancing include organising competitions and providing various support services, usually on a part-time basis.

Community dance

The work involves developing dance within a particular geographical area through teaching or creating dance, or organising others to do so. A full-time dance training or recognised dance teaching qualification is usually required. A full-time community dance course is offered at the Laban Centre, London. Further information can be obtained from the Foundation for Community Dance.

See the section on Teaching Dance for information about dance training.

LEISURE & RECREATION MANAGEMENT

Leisure is a growth industry. All sorts of organisations are involved in providing access to sport and leisure – local authorities, commercial organisations, industrial organisations, universities and colleges, voluntary groups and trusts. So, if you want to get into this sort of work, managing the provision of opportunities for children and young people, as well as adults, you'll need to be really keen.

Managers in the leisure and recreation industry need to be willing and able to take on a varied workload, and – like their staff – work in the evenings and at weekends when necessary. Young people and children form by far the largest client group, so managers within this industry have to feel confident and happy with this age group.

Sports and leisure centres

Large public sports and leisure centres are generally owned by local authorities, but may be run by private operators, or local authority departments. Centres usually have facilities for both indoor and outdoor sports. Some centres have extensive facilities, including pools, sports halls, fitness suites, bars and eating areas – and perhaps an ice rink and arts facilities. Such a centre could employ a number of staff at supervisory and management levels. In contrast, a small local authority sports centre with a pool and dry sports facilities might have a manager working with two assistants. The manager's responsibilities would include recruiting staff, promoting events, organising advertising, managing the finances, health and safety and ensuring the smooth operation of the centre on a daily basis.

The Sports Council runs a number of national sports centres, with facilities for participants in top-level sport. They cater mainly for coaches, officials and national teams, but also host events and have facilities for general and basic courses. Managers are employed to take responsibility for the running and development of the centres.

Leisure and fitness clubs

Recent years have seen the growth of privately owned health and fitness clubs and studios, country clubs, leisure clubs attached to hotels and sports clubs offering a range of leisure facilities. Such facilities may include gyms, swimming pools, saunas, bars and restaurants. The manager's responsibilities are similar in many respects to those of a larger sports and leisure facility as previously described. In smaller clubs, the manager may have to get involved in the basic day-to-day operational work, as well as management tasks.

University and college sports centres

Educational establishments often provide very good sports and leisure facilities. Jobs can involve both administrative work and physical education/coaching. A physical education background is usually preferred.

Theme parks and similar leisure facilities

In the commercial sector, there are a growing number of large-scale leisure attractions, incorporating things like fairground-style rides and amusements, animal collections, and exhibitions of all sorts (often on a historical theme). Stately homes have gone into these sorts of ventures in a big way. Holiday centres, such as Pontins, or the newer established Center Parcs, are designed to appeal to the general public and families in particular, trying to provide 'something for everyone'. The job opportunities lie particularly in general and financial **management**, and **marketing** and **promotions** – obviously, some facilities need specialist staff to deal with particular themes or facilities.

Outdoor holiday organisations

These include the Youth Hostels Associations, the Holiday Fellowship, the Countryside Holiday Association, and the Camping Club of Great Britain and Ireland. These organisations provide reasonably priced holiday accommodation and promote outdoor recreational activities such as walking, canoeing, pony-trekking and cycling. Senior posts are very few and vacancies are rare. The requirements are generally for good **administrators** and for specialists such as **surveyors** and **accountants**.

There are also holiday organisations which operate on a strictly commercial basis – e.g. PGL Adventure Holidays and Camp Beaumont. These provide activity holidays for children, teenagers and adults. There are job opportunities (including seasonal openings) for **instructors** and **supervisors**, as well as the usual administrative posts.

Sports development work

The aim of sports development work is to help to promote participation in sport, and to improve sporting excellence. Some jobs involve promoting a particular sport; others are about developing sport in general. Employers include local authorities, regional and national bodies, and the governing bodies of various sports. A great deal of contact with people is involved, such as community groups, the media, people working in local and national government and various other agencies. The work can involve dealing with matters like funding, publicity, events promotion, standards of training, and the development of facilities. The Sports Council, for instance, is the independent body which promotes sport and facilities for physical recreation in England (with similar councils in Scotland, Wales and Northern Ireland), and there are also regional and local sports councils to advise on more local requirements. They are staffed by research, administrative and technical personnel – but not in great numbers.

ENTRY AND TRAINING

There are many ways into careers in leisure and recreation management where you work to promote leisure activities for children and young people. Traditionally it has been a career area where people can work their way up to management level, through gaining experience and studying part-time. Gaining a professional qualification, while rarely absolutely essential, will be very helpful – especially if you wish to progress to more senior positions. As the number of leisure and recreation courses at higher education level grows, it may well become more difficult for people without such qualifications to get started. For some types of work, specialist qualifications are needed, for instance, ability and achievement in sport. Much depends on the individual post.

Part-time courses

Courses can be taken by going to college part-time, or through open learning by studying mainly at home or entirely on your own. Some of the qualifications for which you might study whilst working in relevant employment are:

- Institute of Leisure and Amenity Management qualifications – offer a variety of awards including a new Certificate in Technical Operations, relating to facility plant operations;
- Institute of Sport and Recreation Management qualifications;
- City & Guilds 481 Recreation and Leisure;
- NVQ in Sport and Recreation;
- Certificate of the National Examination Board in Supervisory Management (NEBSM) in Recreation Management;
- BTEC Continuing Education Certificate in Leisure Management leading to entry to the ILAM Certificate in Leisure Management.

Full-time and sandwich courses

Consult handbooks such as the *Directory of Further Education*, or use the ECCTIS database, which may be available in your local careers centre. Courses include Intermediate and Advanced GNVQs in Leisure and Tourism and relevant BTEC Higher National Diplomas.

A degree can be a useful preparation for administrative and managerial posts in recreation/leisure provision. While job opportunities are often open to graduates from a wide range of degree subjects, it is likely that applicants who have degree subjects related to the industry may have an advantage. Relevant subjects include recreation and leisure management, sports science, sports studies and human movement studies. However, employers take a range of factors into consideration, such as experience of organising sports and social events, personal qualities and so on. Consult the various higher education handbooks and the ECCTIS database for suitable courses. The CRAC *Degree Course Guide: Leisure and Sports Studies* is very useful.

Postgraduate and post-experience courses
There are various professional diploma courses and higher degrees in aspects of leisure and recreation management, intended mainly for people with some relevant work experience.

NURSING SICK CHILDREN

Nursing children calls for some special skills – you are caring not only for the child, but also supporting and helping the parents. You can specialise in learning how to nurse sick children after completing the first 18 months of a three-year nursing diploma course. You need at least five GCSEs at grade C (or equivalent qualifications) to begin nursing training, although adults may be able to take an educational entrance test instead.

Most people don't like being in hospital, but a child can find it especially frightening and strange. It is very stressful to be suddenly taken away from your home when you are feeling ill, and then having to have tests or an operation. Parents of young children often stay with their child in hospital, helping with their care and treatment.

Wherever possible, the nursing of sick children takes place both in hospital and at home, so nurses working in the community have a very important role to play with parents, providing them with support, reassurance and clear explanations of any treatment the child is having.

What it takes

In **paediatric nursing** (as children's nursing is called) you learn a lot about child psychology and development. Young children can't always explain how they feel, or where a pain is. Children often develop symptoms more extremely and suddenly than adults. So nurses must learn to be very careful observers, and to be able to interpret behaviour. Nurses must be able to cope with worried and distressed families, as well as being reassuring for the children.

Children's nursing can be very challenging. As well as understanding the special needs of children, children's nurses need all the knowledge and skills that any nurse must have. In the children's ward or children's hospital, the nurses are very much part of a team which includes doctors and consultants, therapists of all kinds (speech, physio-, occupational, play), teachers, and many specialists such as dieticians and radiotherapists.

In terms of personality, you need to be the sort of person who can stay very calm and cool in a crisis. As well as the joy of seeing most children get better, a children's nurse must be able to cope with the distress of helping severely ill or disabled children, and the sadness of having child patients die from time to time.

ENTRY AND TRAINING

For every sort of nursing education you need to be at least $17\frac{1}{2}$ years old. The usual minimum requirement for diploma courses is five GCSEs at grade C (or the equivalent). Some institutions may prefer applicants who have A levels, or they may have particular subject preferences. Mature applicants are very much welcomed and, if you haven't got the five GCSEs, you can ask to take an educational entry test instead. This may particularly apply to older applicants. For degree courses, a minimum of two A levels, or the equivalent, is required – consult individual prospectuses for detailed requirements.

There are some shortened nursing courses for graduates with a related health/scientific degree subject.

Diploma programmes
To gain a diploma in nursing, you take a Common Foundation Programme (CFP) which lasts 18 months, followed by another

18 months of training in one of four branches of nursing. You would choose children's nursing as the branch in which you want to specialise. Student nurses receive a non-means-tested bursary.

Degrees in nursing

A number of degree-level nursing courses that offer the child branch of nursing are available. You would study similar subject areas, but course lengths vary from three to four years. If you are applying for a degree course in nursing, you will need to apply to your local education authority for advice on funding your training.

APPLYING

Applications for diploma courses in England are processed by the Nursing and Midwifery Admissions Service. The NMAS will send you an application package, containing the necessary forms and details of all the institutions offering nursing courses. Applications to universities for degree courses in nursing are handled by UCAS, in the same way as for any other degree course.

Other opportunities for nursing children

Besides jobs in general hospitals, there are opportunities (some very demanding ones) in residential schools and homes for children with special needs, in hospices for children who are terminally ill, and in overseas relief and development work.

Nurses who are trained to specialise in **mental health** can work in the challenging area of nursing children who suffer from mental illness. There is also a lot of scope for nurses with a **learning disability nursing** qualification to work with children of all ages and in a variety of settings, both in hospitals and in the community. See the next section, and the sections on midwifery and community healthcare.

just
THE
JOB

LEARNING DISABILITY NURSING

> Learning disability nursing is very much a mix of caring
> and practical teaching. An important difference between
> this branch of nursing and most others is that you are not
> dealing with ill people who are going to recover. But you
> can help your clients make the most of the abilities which
> they do have, and this makes the job both challenging and
> rewarding.

Learning disability covers a wide range of conditions. Some children have mild learning difficulties, which makes it harder for them than for most people to read, write or solve everyday problems. However, many young people and adults with mild learning difficulties live full lives and hold down a job. At the other end of the scale, there are people who have suffered severe brain damage and will need special care all their lives. Some people with learning disabilities also have physical problems.

What the work involves

A learning disability nurse is, in many ways, more of a teacher than a provider of medical care and treatment. Nurses help people with learning disabilities to live more independent and fuller lives, by providing plenty of mental stimulation and interest.

Learning disability nurses get involved in all sorts of activities which you wouldn't usually think of when nursing is mentioned. Nurses may teach clients to feed and dress themselves, and to learn about the world outside, so that they may be able, in the future, to live in sheltered or independent accommodation. Many learning disability nurses work in the community: for example, with a group of people with learning difficulties who are able to share a house and live quite independently if they are given just that bit of extra support.

Learning disability nurses mainly work as part of a team which includes other health service professionals such as psychologists, physiotherapists, occupational therapists and doctors. During their training, nurses learn to work effectively with these specialists. Learning disability nurses also gain experience of ordinary hospitals while training, so that they know something about general nursing.

What it takes

Learning disability nursing might be the career for you if you:

- are very patient;
- want to work with people in caring way;
- would enjoy working as part of a team;
- would like a branch of nursing where you build up a long-term relationship with your clients, and their families or carers.

GETTING STARTED

For all nursing training, you must be at least $17\frac{1}{2}$ years old before you can start. Many entrants to learning disability work are older than this, and are particularly welcomed, as maturity and relevant experience are important assets. There are two training pathways to becoming a Registered Nurse – through a diploma course or a degree (see previous section).

The **diploma** involves a three-year course involving 18 months of study on a Common Foundation Programme, followed by 18 months following your chosen nursing specialism, which would be the learning disability branch. The programme is a mix of academic study and practical training, and will involve gaining experience alongside trained staff working with people with learning difficulties in various settings in the community.

There are a number of **degree** courses leading to the learning disability nursing qualification, which last three or four years. Two A levels, or the equivalent, are the minimum entry requirements; some courses stipulate that one of the A levels should be a science. Successful applicants are likely to hold more than the minimum requirement. Graduates with health-related or science degrees may be able to enter shortened two-year courses leading to registered nursing qualifications.

If you are a Registered Nurse in a different branch, there are some, although limited, opportunities for training for learning disability nursing.

RETURN TO NURSING

There are ENB short preparation courses for those nurses who have been out of the profession for five years or more, and wish to return. At present, this is a recommendation rather than a requirement.

Healthcare assistant

Healthcare assistants are employed in hospitals and homes for people with learning disabilities. They are not trained nurses, but do basic care work – washing, feeding and dressing patients. They also play an important role in helping patients to be more independent. No educational qualifications are required for this work, and you are trained on-the-job. You may be able to gain NVQs. If you are thinking of entering learning disability nursing, gaining some experience as a healthcare assistant can be useful.

just
THE
JOB

MIDWIFERY

Midwives are professionally qualified to give care and advice to women during pregnancy, labour, delivery, and after having a baby. It is a highly responsible job with a lot of variety, open to both women and men. You can either qualify as a midwife after completing your registered nurse training, or you can choose the direct entry route into midwifery. Nursing or midwifery education normally requires at least five GCSEs at grade C, or equivalent qualifications, and preferably two A levels.

What the work involves
Antenatal care
An expectant mother first meets a midwife either in the antenatal clinic, or in her own home, usually early in pregnancy. She has regular check-ups at the clinic with a midwife and/or doctor or obstetrician. They examine her to make sure that both she and her unborn baby are in good health, and that the baby is developing normally.

Maternity units aim for a high level of continuity of care, but this is generally easier to achieve in small hospitals and maternity units than in the really large ones. The mother may see different midwives at her antenatal check-ups, rather than the same one each time. This is because the midwives generally alternate between working in the antenatal clinic, and on the labour and postnatal wards (or in the community). If the mother is booked for a home birth, she will be under the care of the **community midwife** and will generally have more continuity of care.

Meeting several midwives during her pregnancy does increase the mother's chances of knowing the midwife who happens to be on duty when she goes into labour, and the staff who will care for her after the birth. As antenatal visits get more frequent towards the end of pregnancy, each midwife can get to know the mother quite well. Part of the antenatal care involves discussing with the mother the sort of birth she hopes to have – how she feels about the prospect of labour, about her attitudes towards high-tech equipment, different sorts of pain relief, and so on.

Another aspect of antenatal care in which midwives can get involved is education for parenthood – teaching groups of expectant mothers and fathers about labour and giving birth, and how to care for the baby in the early days.

Delivering babies

These days, most babies are born in hospital, although in recent years there has been a greater demand for home births. Normal deliveries of babies are carried out by midwives acting on their own. When everything is straightforward, there is no doctor in attendance. But, of course, the midwife must be able to recognise the warning signs of impending difficulties, and know when a doctor's involvement is necessary. If a doctor is unavailable, for whatever reason, midwives need to be able to carry out emergency measures themselves.

The midwife works closely and unobtrusively with the mother in labour, and with the father of the baby, to help them achieve the sort of birth they want. The mother is consulted about her wishes, given choices whenever possible, and kept informed at all times about what is happening. The midwife is an important source of emotional and psychological support, as well as being an 'expert' in her field.

Midwives find great pleasure in the birth of a healthy baby. But there is also a sad side to the job, and they must learn to help

their clients cope with miscarriages, stillbirths and births of babies with severe disabilities, which happen from time to time.

Postnatal care

On postnatal wards and in the community, midwives make sure the mother is recovering properly from the birth, and that the baby is in good health. The midwives advise on feeding the baby, whether by breast or bottle, and on general baby care. Some ill and very small babies – usually born several weeks before their expected delivery date – go into special care units. Caring for them is one specialism open to midwives and other nurses.

An important part of postnatal work is giving the mother emotional support in her new role. Facing up to full responsibility for a first baby in particular can be very daunting, physically and mentally, especially if the mother is tired and not fully fit following the birth. Postnatal depression is quite a common occurrence which has to be watched out for. At times, the midwife has to liaise with other professionals if the mother and baby have difficult home conditions.

These days, mothers have only a short stay in hospital after their baby's birth, even if it is their first child. Some go home within just a few hours of the birth, although a three- to five-day stay is more common. Once they are home, mother and baby are the **community midwife's** responsibility for ten days (perhaps up to 28 days) of the baby's life, before the health visitor takes over. The community midwife normally visits at least once a day to start with to see that everything is all right.

What it takes

A good midwife is someone who:

- is kind, observant and self-reliant – not the sort of person who is short-tempered, or flaps in a crisis;
- is able to communicate well with all sorts of people and can put people at their ease;
- has a certain level of maturity and an understanding of human relationships;
- can work well as part of a team;
- can keep accurate records and reports.

WORKING CONDITIONS

Midwives can work in the very modern maternity units of large hospitals, in smaller hospitals which have midwife-led units for straightforward deliveries, in private hospitals and maternity homes, in the community, for agencies, or as self-employed practitioners.

Most midwives are hospital-based, although the trend is for more midwives to be community-based. They work shifts, and can rotate between antenatal, labour/delivery and postnatal care so that they keep up-to-date with all their skills. However, the way in which their work is organised does vary from one area to another.

At least a fifth of all midwives work in the community.

Community midwives work between a number of bases – hospitals, GP surgeries and health centres, antenatal clinics – and are often on the road between one home visit and the next. In the community, the hours worked are basically daytime hours, but midwives in a particular area take it in turns to be on call at night and to cover weekends.

There are part-time and job-share opportunities in midwifery, and you may also have the chance to work, for example, permanent nights, or days only in antenatal clinics. If you work for an agency or as a **freelance midwife**, you may have more choice over the hours you work.

EDUCATION AND TRAINING

To practise as a midwife, you have to be registered with the United Kingdom Central Council. The qualification is RM – **Registered Midwife**. You can achieve this through going on a specialised course leading straight to a midwifery qualification – a route which is becoming increasingly popular – or by first qualifying as a registered nurse, and then following post-registration training in midwifery.

The direct route: diploma level
A three-year higher education diploma course in midwifery leads directly to qualified midwife status. The minimum age to begin midwife education is $17\frac{1}{2}$ and there is no upper age limit – mature entrants are welcomed. Applicants must normally have five GCSEs at grade C (or the equivalent) which have to include English language and science, and preferably two A levels. Entry is very competitive, and most colleges will require more than the minimum qualifications. Contact the ENB for details of colleges offering courses and how to apply for training. People without the minimum qualifications can take an educational test at the discretion of the particular institution – this may apply to older applicants in particular.

The direct route: degree level

Direct training through a three- or four-year degree course is also possible. You will gain both a degree and a registered midwife qualification at the end of the course. You study midwifery, alongside courses in the social and biological sciences. Entry requirements are usually a minimum of two A levels, preferably including a science subject. Supporting GCSEs should include English, mathematics and science. Alternative, but equivalent, qualifications are equally acceptable for degree course entry.

Mature applicants without such qualifications should contact degree course admissions tutors for advice. Access courses at a college of further education can be a useful route for mature entrants. A list of universities offering study courses for the midwifery qualification in combination with a degree programme is available from the ENB.

Note: The degree course is becoming the preferred route for the Royal College of Midwives. Because of the academic qualifications required to start the course, students cope better with the high academic content of the work.

Training after qualifying as a Registered Nurse

People who have completed a nursing diploma through the adult branch (taking three years), can then qualify as a midwife by taking a further course lasting 18 months. There is no need to train as a midwife straight after qualifying as a nurse. Many people first gain some general nursing experience. Nurses who have taken a break in their careers can re-enter by training in midwifery. Check with individual institutions for advice.

PROSPECTS FOR QUALIFIED MIDWIVES

Once qualified, midwives can gain experience in the many aspects of maternal and neonatal care. There are opportunities for promotion, and courses leading to advanced qualifications.

There are also opportunities to specialise in the clinical or managerial fields, or to go into research or teaching.

UK midwifery qualifications are acceptable within the European Union, throughout the Commonwealth and in various other countries, so there are good opportunities for overseas employment. Voluntary work and paid employment in developing countries are other areas where midwives and midwifery teachers are welcomed and can do valuable work.

Note: If you are considering training by the direct route to midwifery, you should be aware that your qualification will be as a Registered Midwife, not as a Registered Nurse. You would not be qualified for entry to professional training such as health visiting, practice nursing or other specialisms for which a Registered Nurse qualification is essential. If you choose the direct route to qualification as a midwife, you need to be sure that midwifery is your particular area of interest. As a qualified midwife, however, a range of continuing education courses and opportunities for career progression, related to your chosen field, will be open to you.

COMMUNITY HEALTHCARE

> M ore healthcare is now managed in the community, including within people's own homes. District nurses and health visitors are in the forefront of this sort of caring. They are qualified nurses who undertake further training. Nurse education normally requires at least five GCSEs at grade C or equivalent.

District nurse

District nurses care for patients, of any age group, who do not need to be in hospital but still require skilled nursing. This includes:

- people with long-term or terminal illnesses who are being cared for at home by their family, under their GP and the district nursing team;
- working with acute hospital discharges following surgery;
- visiting children who need treatment to be given or supervised;
- giving advice, help and support to the families who are caring for them.

District nurses are usually part of a community healthcare team, which includes nurses, health visitors, social workers and care assistants. They may work as part of a medical practice, providing treatment at a surgery or health centre and working with the doctors in the practice; or outside the health service, working for private nursing agencies.

Most district nursing jobs are full-time and involve doing day work on a rota basis. Nurses take turns to work at weekends, and on public holidays. There are also part-time opportunities, and jobs with evening/night nursing teams. These teams provide an evening care service to patients (they change dressings and put patients to bed, for instance). They are also available on emergency call-out if there's a crisis in the night.

This is a very responsible job, where you work independently, and it can be hard work. Nursing people in their own homes can mean a lot of physical handling, often with no one to help with the lifting. You also need to build up good relationships with the patients' families, especially with terminally-ill patients. There is quite a lot of travelling, and district nurses normally need to be able to drive and to own a car, for which they get an allowance when they are using it for work.

Health visitor

Promoting health and preventing ill health is the main concern of health visitors, and much of their time is spent on work with families with babies and young children. They also work with elderly people and people with disabilities in the community. Health visitors generally work from a surgery where a number of general practitioners (family doctors) work together, and have responsibility for the patients of that practice; some may work from a health centre. There may be opportunities for part-time work or job sharing.

Child health, welfare and development are very important to the community as a whole. Health visitors play their part by making sure that babies are developing properly. They visit all new babies in their homes, assess their development and advise and support parents. Health visitors are a very helpful source of advice on childcare, feeding and behaviour problems. It is very important to form good relationships with parents, working with them to help them make informed decisions.

Working with babies and young children takes the health visitor into the homes of the families in his or her care. Visits take place following a programme agreed with the family. The health visitor also sees parents and children in baby clinics, where, in an informal atmosphere, they can come for health checks and weighing, or just for advice and a chat about how the baby is getting on. Parents' clubs and classes are also run for new and expectant mums and dads, and health visitors also get involved with playgroups, mother and toddler clubs, day nurseries, and childminders.

Of course, the health visitor sometimes comes across families in which there are problems. When they meet problems like child abuse, poverty or poor housing, they act as a referral agency to other organisations such as the social services department. In turn, they work with social services departments and other statutory and voluntary organisations to support and help families with difficulties. Health visitors have a very important role to play in identifying families where children may be at risk, and helping to prevent neglect and ill-treatment. They may have to be persistent to see any children that they suspect to be at risk.

Health visitors work in the wider community, promoting good health by talking to all age groups. The health visitor has an important role working with families, supporting and counselling in times of stress, knowing when to refer to the appropriate helping agencies, promoting good health and the early detection of ill health and disease. Working with elderly people, health visitors are concerned to help them to maintain a good quality of life. They assess their physical, social and emotional health, and make sure they know about common problems such as hypothermia, malnutrition and depression, and how to prevent them.

QUALIFICATIONS AND TRAINING

District nurses and health visitors are fully qualified Registered Nurses, with about two years of general nursing experience.

The post-registration full-time courses last a year; the part-time courses last two years or longer. All courses lead to a degree level qualification. Trainees are generally sponsored by a community health trust.

Your starting point, therefore, is to qualify as a registered nurse. To start on nurse training, you will need at least five GCSEs at grade C, or equivalent qualifications. If you don't have GCSEs, you can ask to take an entry test instead. Degree courses in nursing are also available, for which you will need two or three A levels or equivalent (see previous section).

Other community nursing opportunities

With the move towards more healthcare being delivered in the community, rather than within hospitals, there is a growing range of opportunities for nurses of all backgrounds to work in the community in some capacity.

Paediatric nurses (who work with children) work in the community health team; **mental health nurses** are usually attached to the community care department of their local psychiatric unit or hospital; **learning disability nurses** care for people who have learning disabilities living in the community; **community midwives** care for mothers and babies who have either been born at home, or who go home from hospital within ten days of birth; **practice nurses** are based at GPs' surgeries, dealing with routine work like taking blood tests, giving vaccinations, changing dressings, and are involved in health promotion; **school nurses** have responsibility for the well-being of pupils.

SPEECH & LANGUAGE THERAPY

Speech and language therapy helps adults and children to overcome communication problems. Trained therapists work in a variety of settings, which include hospitals, schools, community clinics and private practice. You need a degree or postgraduate qualification in speech and language therapy to work in this field. There are some opportunities to work at assistant level.

What is speech and language therapy?

Communication is very important in the way we function as human beings and interpret the world around us. To suddenly lose the power of speech, or never to have developed it properly, can be tremendously damaging to a person's psychological state, as well as making it difficult for them to take an active part in society.

Perhaps the most familiar example of a speech problem is stammering. Speech and language therapists also have to deal with a variety of other conditions which are often complex and difficult to treat. Children may need speech and language therapy for a variety of reasons, such as learning difficulties, deafness or a cleft palate, and it is important that they receive this help early, as psychological problems can develop from an inability to communicate. Some children, or adults, may learn to communicate using an electronic communication aid, a symbol chart or sign language. Speech and language therapists also deal with other related problems, such as the inability to swallow.

Problems of this kind are not easily or quickly overcome. The therapy may last weeks, months or even years. The satisfaction of the job for a therapist comes from seeing a steady, if slow, improvement in their client's condition.

Clients are referred to speech and language therapists by health visitors, GPs, teachers or hospital consultants.

What it takes

Speech and language therapists need:

- good hearing and clear speech;
- to be well organised;
- a friendly and patient manner to build up their clients' confidence and skill;
- sympathy with the problems of their patients;
- an ability to make their own assessment of a client's condition and decide on a suitable treatment plan for the individual;
- imagination to devise different activities to stimulate the patients;
- to be able to communicate well with the client's family, and members of their own medical team.

In hospitals and clinics, speech and language therapists work closely with nurses, doctors, social workers and the patients' families. Some jobs may involve being in one centre all the time; others may involve a considerable amount of travelling, perhaps around a number of schools, or to clients' homes. For travelling jobs, you may need to be able to drive.

WORKING CONDITIONS

There is a career structure for speech and language therapists, with senior posts involving specific responsibilities and/or managerial responsibility. There also a limited number of teaching jobs on speech and language therapy courses. Other therapists may go into research.

Speech and language therapists often work long hours because of the volume and pressure of work, but there is some scope for part-time work. Pay can be compared with national average rates for graduate jobs.

The first job after training is usually in a post where a wide range of work is undertaken. It is possible to specialise later in a particular type of work, although additional training may be necessary.

QUALIFICATIONS AND TRAINING

All speech and language therapy training is now through degree courses lasting three or four years, or a two-year postgraduate diploma or masters degree. Funding for degree level courses is through your local education authority, as for any degree course. Educational establishments running postgraduate courses may be able to advise on sources of funding for courses at this level.

Course titles include *speech and language therapy*, *clinical communication studies*, *speech pathology and therapy* and *speech sciences*. Subjects covered include language, voice, speech and hearing, anatomy and physiology, phonetics and linguistics, neurology, psychology and child development.

Entry to courses is very competitive. The minimum academic qualifications needed to achieve a place on a course are five GCSEs at grade C, plus two A levels. Three A levels are likely to be preferred. Advanced GNVQ or a BTEC National Diploma may also be acceptable, as may two AS levels in place of one A level; check with individual institutions. In practice, an extra A level with an Advanced GNVQ would be highly desirable. At GCSE, required subjects can include English, a science subject, mathematics and a modern language. At A level, preferred subjects include biology or another science subject; some courses do not specify particular subjects. Each course sets its own requirements for essential or preferred subjects, and these do vary, so it is important check with individual institutions. Besides those subjects already mentioned, music and psychology are also relevant.

A full list of courses with entry requirements is available from the Royal College of Speech and Language Therapists (see Further Information section).

Assistant level work

Opportunities for working as a speech and language therapist's assistant are now widespread. Assistants can work with the whole range of client groups, but in particular may be found working with clients with learning disabilities and with children. Duties vary according to the situation, and experience of the assistant, but can include everything from helping clients with basic care needs, through to assisting with speech exercises.

Entry qualifications may not be essential, but each employer sets their own requirements. Personality and maturity is important. People enter from a wide range of backgrounds. Many of the jobs are part-time, and some operate on a term-time only basis. An NVQ in Speech and Language Therapy Support is available, as part of the level 3 NVQ in Care. For further information, contact the Royal College of Speech and Language Therapists.

just
THE
JOB

SPECIALISATIONS IN MEDICINE

Thoughts of a medical career bring to mind images of a GP or a surgeon in the operating theatre, but there are many other specialties open to the newly trained doctor, some of which offer opportunities to work specifically with children and young people. Specialist training for most branches of medicine and surgery can start one year after graduating, though doctors often choose to gain some broad experience first, before following a more selective path of learning.

Generally, after first gaining your basic medical qualification, it will take seven or eight years, with further exams, before a doctor can hope to become a consultant (the senior post in a hospital department). The average age for obtaining a first post as a consultant is around 35.

Competition for some specialties is much more intense than for others. The choice of specialty is likely to depend not only on personal interests, but also on career prospects and the opportunities which present themselves. Because becoming fully-trained in the specialty of one's choice takes such a long time, intending doctors who plan to take some time out to look after their own children are especially advised to plan their career pattern carefully.

Some part-time training is available in all the major specialties, especially in shortage areas like anaesthetics and psychiatry. It is less easy to find with the more popular specialties and with those areas where, because of the high level of emergency work, part-time training becomes difficult.

Medical specialties

In hospitals, there is a wide range of specialties under the general heading of medicine, including paediatrics (illnesses of children) and psychiatry – the child and adolescent branch. A newly-graduated doctor will gain experience in various branches of medicine during the pre-registration year, which will help in the choice of specialty.

Paediatrics

This is one of the major and most popular branches of medicine and is concerned with children from the newborn or neo-natal stage up to puberty. Advances are constantly being made and the paediatrician can specialise in various areas. The scope of the work includes research into genetics, causes of unexpected death in very young children, the treatment of sick children and those with disabilities. They also work on abnormalities from birth which, though once irreversible, may now be corrected by biochemical and other treatments. Jobs vary from research-based posts to those where there is much involvement both with young patients and with their families.

Psychiatry

Not to be confused with psychology, psychiatry is a branch of medicine which deals with mental health and development, and the medical treatment of mental disorders. Only psychiatrists may prescribe drugs and treatments such as electro-convulsive therapy. Psychiatrists are also trained to provide treatments based on psychotherapy and behaviour therapy, for individuals, families and groups.

The number of hospital beds occupied by psychiatric patients has decreased as more and more people are being treated while living in the community. Psychiatrists who have first gained a general psychiatric training – usually at least three years after basic qualification as a doctor – can then specialise in child and adolescent psychiatry, one of six possible routes.

Many other medical workers spend a proportion of their time with children and young people, whilst carrying the full age range within their patient listings. This includes the occupational areas:

- chiropodist/podiatrist – specialising in the care of feet;
- optometrist – testing sight and prescribing spectacles and contact lenses;
- orthoptist – diagnosing and treating eye problems (eg squints);
- dentist/dental therapist and hygienist;
- dental nurse;
- doctor;
- sport physiotherapist;
- radiographer/radiotherapist;
- dietician.

More detail about these career areas can be found in *Medicine & Health* in the *Just the Job!* series.

146

FOR FURTHER INFORMATION

CHILDCARE & NURSERY NURSING

Association of Nursery Training Colleges – The Princess
   Christian College, 26 Wilbraham Road, Fallowfield,
   Manchester M14 6JX. Tel: 0161 224 4560.

**CACHE (Council for Awards in Children's Care and
   Education)** – 8 Chequer Street, St Albans, Hertfordshire AL1
   3XZ. Tel: 01727 847636. Provides details on the CACHE
   courses.

**NAMCW – The National Association for Maternal and
   Child Welfare Ltd** – First Floor, 40-42 Osnaburgh Street,
   London NW1 3ND. Tel: 0171 383 4541.

National Association of Nursery Nurses – 12 The Wayside,
   Hurworth on Tees, Darlington, County Durham DL2 2EE.
   Tel: 01325 720511.

Professional Association of Nursery Nurses – 2 St James's
   Court, Friar Gate, Derby DE1 1BT. Tel: 01332 343029.
   Provides leaflets giving guidelines for nannies; advice on setting
   up a day nursery, etc.

The Children's Society – Edward Rudolf House, 69–85
   Margery Street, London WC1X 0JL. Tel: 0171 837 4299.

Private colleges

Agency for Jewish Education – 44 Albert Road, Hendon,
   London NW4 2SJ, offers a diploma course especially tailored to
   meet the requirements of the Jewish community.

Chiltern Nursery Training College – 16 Peppard Road,
   Caversham, Reading, Berkshire RG4 8JZ.

London Montessori Centre – 18 Balderton Street, London
   W1Y 1TG.

Maria Montessori Training Organisation – 26 Lyndhurst
   Gardens, London NW3 5NW.

The Norland College – Denford Park, Hungerford, Berkshire RG17 0PQ.
Princess Christian College – 26 Wilbraham Road, Fallowfield, Manchester M14 6JX.

Careers Working with Children and Young People, published by Kogan Page.
Working in Work with Children, published by COIC.

NANNY, PARENT'S HELP & AU PAIR
The Au Pair and Nanny's Guide to Working Abroad, published by Vacation Work.
A Year Off ... A Year On?, published by Lifetime Careers Wiltshire.
Taking a Year Out, by Polly Bird, published by Hodder & Stoughton.

CHILDMINDING & FOSTERING
Barnardo's – Tanners Lane, Barkingside, Ilford, Essex IG6 1QG. Tel: 0181 550 8822.
National Childminding Association – 8 Masons Hill, Bromley, Kent BR2 9EY. Tel: 0181 464 6164. Produces a range of publications giving advice on all aspects of childminding.
National Foster Care Association – Leonard House, 5-7 Marshalsea Road, London SE1 1EP. Tel: 0171 828 6266. Issues free information pack on fostering.
NCH Action for Children – 85 Highbury Park, London N5 1UD. Tel: 0171 226 2033.

The Lady (published Fridays) is the best source of job advertisements placed by private households and families. There are also employment agencies, mainly in large cities, which specialise in finding domestic staff. They also advertise in *The Lady*.

You could approach the education department of your local authority for further information.

HAPA: Adventure Play for Children with Disabilities and Special Needs – Pryor's Bank, Bishop's Park, London SW6 3LA. Tel: 0171 731 1435.

Kids Club Network – Bellerive House, 3 Muirfield Crescent, London E14 9SZ. Tel: 0171 512 2112.

National Centre for Playwork Education – *London*: Block D, Barnsbury Park Complex, Offord Road, London N1 1QG. Tel: 0171 457 5824; *South West*: Cheltenham and Gloucester College of Higher Education, Hardwick Campus, St Paul's Road, Cheltenham, Gloucestershire GL50 4BS. Tel: 01242 532949; *North East*: Kielder House, University of Northumbria, Coach Lane Campus, Benton, Newcastle-upon-Tyne NE7 7XA. Tel: 0191 227 4604; *West Midlands*: Westhill College, Weoley Park Road, Selly Oak, Birmingham, West Midlands B29 6LL. Tel: 0121 415 2227.

National Play Information Centre – 199 Knightsbridge, London SW7 1DE. Tel: 0171 584 6464.

Play-Train – 31 Farm Road, Birmingham B11 1LS. Tel: 0121 766 8446.

Playlink – The Co-op Centre, Unit 5, 11 Mowll Street, London SW9 6BG. Tel: 0171 820 3800.

Spirito (The Specialist Industry Training Organisation for Sport, Recreation, Playwork, Outdoor Education & Development Training) – Euston House, 81–103 Euston Street, London NW1 2ET. Tel: 0171 388 3111.

The awarding bodies for NVQs in Playwork:

BTEC – Edexcel Foundation, Central House, Upper Woburn Place, London WC1H 0HH. Tel: 0171 413 8400.

CACHE (Council for Awards in Children's Care and Education) – 8 Chequer Street, St Albans, Hertfordshire AL1 3XZ. Tel: 01727 847636.

City & Guilds – 1 Giltspur Street, London EC1A 9DD. Tel: 0171 294 2468.

RSA – Progress House, Westwood Business Park, Westwood Way, Coventry CV4 8HS. Tel: 01203 470033.

Scottish Qualifications Authority – Ironmills Road, Dalkeith, Midlothian, EH22 1LE. Tel: 0131 663 6601.

SOCIAL WORK

Central Council for Education and Training in Social Work (CCETSW) – Derbyshire House, St Chad's Street, London WC1H 8AD. Tel: 0171 278 2455. Detailed information can be obtained from CCETSW.

Central Council for Education and Training in Social Work (CCETSW) Cymru – Information Service, 2nd Floor, West Wing, South Gate House, Wood Street, Cardiff CF1 1EW. Tel: 01222 226257.

SWAS (Social Work Admissions System) – Fulton House, Jessop Avenue, Cheltenham, Gloucestershire GL50 3SH. Tel: 01242 225977.

Working in Social Work, published by COIC.

Social Work and Probation Work is an AGCAS graduate careers information booklet available from CSU, Despatch Department, Armstrong House, Oxford Road, Manchester M1 7ED. Tel: 0161 236 9816 ext 250/251.

YOUTH WORK

National Youth Agency – 17-23 Albion Street, Leicester LE1 6GD. Tel: 0116 285 6789.

Youth Clubs UK – 11 St Bride Street, London EC4A 4AS. Tel: 0171 353 2366.

YMCA – 640 Forest Road, Walthamstow, London E17 3DZ. Tel: 0181 520 5599.

YWCA – Clarendon House, 52 Cornmarket Street, Oxford OX1 3EJ. Tel: 01865 726110.

The NYA Guide to Initial Training Courses in Youth and Community Work is available from the National Youth Agency (address above).

NYA Guide to Becoming a Youth Worker is also obtainable from the National Youth Agency.

Vacancies are advertised in the *Times Educational Supplement*, *Young People Now* and sometimes in the national press – especially in the *Guardian*.

Association of Child Psychotherapists – 120 West Heath Road, London NW3 7TU. Tel: 0181 458 1609.

Association of Educational Psychologists – 3 Sunderland Road, Gilesgate, Durham DH1 2LH. Tel: 0191 384 9512.

British Psychological Society – St Andrew's House, 48 Princess Road East, Leicester LE1 7DR. Tel: 0116 254 9568. Publishes a range of booklets and books concerning training and careers using psychology, such as *Putting Psychology to Work* and *Career Choices in Psychology*.

Which Psychology Degree Course?, published by the British Psychological Society, explains the scope of psychology and provides information on careers and courses.

The CRAC *Degree Course Guide: Psychology* provides a useful introduction to the various courses available.

COUNSELLING

British Association for Counselling – 1 Regent Place, Rugby, Warwickshire CV21 2PJ. Information line: 01788 578328. A free information booklet on counselling and available training and a publications catalogue can be sent on receipt of an A4 stamped, addressed envelope.

CAREERS ADVISORY WORK

College of Guidance Studies – College Road, Hextable, Swanley, Kent BR8 7RN. Tel: 01322 664407.

Institute of Careers Guidance – 27a Lower High Street, Stourbridge, West Midlands DY8 1TA. Tel: 01384 376464. Services include providing vacancy information covering a wide range of opportunities in careers guidance.

Local Government Management Board – Layden House, 76–86 Turnmill Street, Faringdon, London EC1M 5QU. Tel: 0171 296 6600 for further details of careers service work, and of courses leading to the DipCG and of centres accrediting NVQs.

PROBATION WORK

Contact the Headquarters of your local probation service – you'll find the address and phone number in the telephone directory – or contact the Home Office at:

Probation Service Division – C6 Division, Home Office, 50 Queen Anne's Gate, London SW1H 9AT. Tel: 0171 273 2675.

National Association of Probation Officers (NAPO) – 4 Chivalry Road, London SW11 1HT. Tel: 0171 223 4887.

Working in Social Work, published by COIC.

Social Work and Probation Work and *Community Work and Advice Work* are AGCAS graduate occupational booklets available from CSU, Armstrong House, Oxford Road, Manchester M1 7ED. Tel: 0161 236 9816, ext 250/251.

CHARITY WORK

Charity Appointments – Longcroft House, Victoria Avenue, London EC2M 4NS. Tel: 0171 623 9292. Publish a booklet *Working for Charities*.

Charity Recruitment – 40 Rosebery Avenue, London EC1R 4RN. Tel: 0171 833 0770.

Institute of Charity Fundraising Managers – 5th Floor, Market Towers, 1 Nine Elms Lane, London SW8 5NQ. Tel: 0171 627 3436.

How to Work for a Charity and *The Directory of Volunteering and Employment Opportunities* can be obtained from the publisher: Directory of Social Change, 24 Stephenson Way, London NW1 2DP. Tel: 0171 209 5151.

VOLUNTARY WORK

National Centre for Volunteering – Carriage Row, 183 Eversholt Street, London NW1 1BU. Tel: 0171 388 9888.

National Council for Voluntary Organisations – Regents Wharf, 8 All Saints Street, London N1 9RL. Tel: 0171 713 6161.

Ilex (Paralegal Training) Ltd – Kempston Manor, Kempston, Bedford MK42 7AB. Tel: 01234 840902. Offer courses leading to the Certificate in Charity Administration and the Diploma in Charity Legacy Administration.

Voluntary Agencies Directory, published by the National Council for Voluntary Organisations, is available from Hamilton House Mailing, 17 Staveley Way, Brixworth Industrial Park, Northampton NN6 9TX. Tel: 01604 881889.
Working in the Voluntary Sector, published by COIC.

TEACHING

Teacher Training Agency – Communication Centre, PO Box 3210, Chelmsford, Essex CM1 3WA. Tel: 01245 454454. Contact for a range of information about teaching and teacher training. Internet: http://www.teach.org.uk

Graduate Teacher Training Registry – Fulton House, Jessop Avenue, Cheltenham, Glos GL50 3SH. Tel: 01242 544788. Publishes a guide to PGCE courses and processes applications.

Maria Montessori Training Organisation – 26 Lyndhurst Gardens, London NW3 5NW. Tel: 0171 435 3646.

Steiner Schools Fellowship – Kidbrooke Park, Forest Row, East Sussex RH18 5JB. Tel: 01342 822115.

Handbook of Initial Teacher Training, published annually by NATFHE, is a directory of teacher training courses.
Working in Teaching, published by COIC.
Careers in Teaching, by Felicity Taylor, published by Kogan Page.
Teaching in Schools and Colleges in the UK, an AGCAS booklet for graduate careers, available from CSU, Despatch Department, Armstrong House, Oxford Road, Manchester M1 7ED. Tel: 0161 236 9816, ext. 250/251.
Applying for Teacher Training – Advice on Applications and Interviews for PGCE courses, published by AGCAS (address above).

See the *Times Educational Supplement* (Fridays) for an idea of vacancies and the sorts of issues which are of concern to educationists.

MUSEUM EDUCATIONAL WORK

Association of Independent Museums – London Transport Museum, 39 Wellington Street, Covent Garden, London WC2E 7BB. Tel: 0171 379 6344.

Department of Museum Studies – University of Leicester, 105 Princess Road East, Leicester LEI 7LG. Tel: 0116 2523 962 for postgraduate information.

Museum Training Institute – 1st Floor, Glyde House, Glydegate, Bradford BD5 0UP. Tel: 01274 391056.

Museums Association – 42 Clerkenwell Close, London EC1R 0PA. Tel: 0171 608 2933.

Museums & Galleries Commission – 16 Queen Anne's Gate, London SW1H 9AA. Tel: 0171 233 4200.

Museums Journal and *Museums Yearbook* can be obtained from the Museums Association (above).

Heritage management and museum work – an AGCAS careers information booklet for graduates, available from CSU, Despatch Department, Armstrong House, Oxford Road, Manchester M1 7ED. Tel: 0161 236 9816, ext 250/251.

Careers in Museums is a very useful booklet, available from the Museum Training Institute at the above address.

TEACHING SPORT & PE

Central Council of Physical Recreation – Francis House, Francis Street, London SW1P 1DE. Tel: 0171 828 3163.

Physical Education Association of the United Kingdom (PEA UK) – Suite 5, 10 Churchill Square, Kings Hill, West Malling, Kent ME19 4DU. Tel: 01732 875888. Can supply careers information on receipt of a stamped, addressed envelope. Also produces a priced booklet – *The Way Forward* – describing careers in physical education, sport and recreation.

Sports Council – 16 Upper Woburn Place, London WC1H 0QP. Tel: 0171 273 1500. Produces *Guide to Education and Training Courses*.

Central Council of Physical Recreation – Francis House, Francis Street, London SW1P 1DE. Tel: 0171 828 3163. Produce a leaflet on movement and dance with contact addresses.

Council for Dance Education & Training (UK) – Riverside Studios, Crisp Road, London W6 9RL. Tel: 0181 741 5084. Will provide general information and a list of accredited courses on receipt of a stamped, addressed envelope.

International Dance Teachers' Association – International House, 76 Bennett Road, Brighton BN2 5JL. Tel: 01273 685652.

MUSIC

Incorporated Society of Musicians (ISM) – 10 Stratford Place, London W1N 9AE. Tel: 0171 629 4413.

Musicians' Union – 60–62 Clapham Road, London SW9 0JJ. Tel: 0171 582 5566.

Sound Sense – Riverside House, Rattlesden, Bury St Edmund, Suffolk IP30 0SF. Tel: 01449 736287. Produces several publications on working in community music, including the quarterly *Sounding Board*. Sound Sense also runs the National Music and Disability Information Service.

British Music Education Yearbook – includes a list of courses, from Rhinegold Publishing.

Music Teacher's Yearbook and *The Musician's Handbook*, available from Rhinegold Publishing.

Careers with Music, a useful and detailed booklet, is available free from the Incorporated Society of Musicians (address above).

The First 10 Years and *Approaching an Agent* are information sheets published by ISM, who also issues the monthly *Music Journal*. Please send a label with your name and address on it, when requesting publications.

NON-TEACHING JOBS IN SCHOOLS

Posts are usually advertised in the local press, but it is sometimes worth approaching heads of schools, particularly for jobs like midday supervisor and education support assistant, to find out about opportunities.

For school and college addresses, look in the telephone directory under the local education authority – or under the name of individual independent schools. Bursars, matrons and assistant matrons, and other jobs in independent schools, are usually advertised in the national press. For assistant matron posts you could contact the recruitment section of Gabbitas Educational Consultants Ltd, Carrington House, 126-130 Regent Street, London W1R 6EE. Tel: 0171 734 0161.

Working In Libraries

Library Association – Information Services, 7 Ridgmount Street, London WC1E 7AE. Tel: 0171 636 7543. Publishes useful, free careers information on *Where to study in the UK, Your move ahead, Financial assistance for study, Qualifications for library assistants* and *Graduate training opportunities*.

Careers In Outdoor Pursuits

National Association for Outdoor Education – 12 St Andrew's Churchyard, Penrith, Cumbria CA11 7YE. Tel: 01768 865113.

British Canoe Union – Adbolton Lane, West Bridgford, Nottingham NG2 5AS. Tel: 0115 9821 100.

British Mountaineering Council – 177-179 Burton Road, West Didsbury, Manchester M20 2BB. Tel: 0161 445 4747.

British Sub-Aqua Club – Telford's Quay, Ellesmere Port, South Wirral, Cheshire L65 4FY. Tel: 0151 357 1951.

English Ski Council – Area Library Building, Queensway Mall, The Cornbow, Halesowen, West Midlands B63 4AJ. Tel: 0121 501 2314.

National Cycling Centre – Manchester Velodrome, Stuart Street, Manchester M11 4DQ. Tel: 0161 223 2244.

Outward Bound Trust – PO Box 1219, Windsor, Berks SL4 1XR. Tel: 01753 731005.

Royal Yachting Association – RYA House, Romsey Road, Eastleigh, Hampshire SO50 9YA. Tel: 01723 627400. Produces a free leaflet on careers in sailing.

Careers in Sport, published by Kogan Page.
Working in Sport and Fitness, published by COIC.

ENTERTAINING & SHOW BUSINESS
British Actors' Equity Association – Guild House, Upper St Martin's Lane, London WC2H 9EG. Tel: 0171 379 6000.
Circomedia – Kingswood Foundation, Britannia Road, Kingswood, Bristol BS15 2DB. Tel 0117 947 7288. Contact Kim Lawrence (administrator) for course details and their basic fund-raising package which advises students on how to find money for their fees, such as career development loans or the Skillsplus scheme.
The Puppet Centre – BAC, Lavender Hill, London SW11 5TN. Tel: 0171 228 5335.

Contacts – an annual directory of courses, venues, agents, contacts and events in the world of theatre and entertainment, published by Spotlight, 7 Leicester Place, London WC2H 7BP. Tel: 0171 437 7631.
Working in Performing Arts, published by COIC.
Careers in the Theatre, published by Kogan Page.
Working in Performing Arts, published by COIC.
The Stage – weekly from newsagents.

DRAMA & ACTING
British Actors' Equity Association – Guild House, Upper St Martin's Lane, London WC2H 9EG. Tel: 0171 379 6000.
Conference of Drama Schools – c/o The Central School of Speech and Drama, Embassy Theatre, Eton Avenue, London NW3 3HY. Tel: 0171 722 8183. Publishes the annual *Guide to Drama Training*.
National Council for Drama Training – 5 Tavistock Place, London WC1H 9SN. Tel: 0171 387 3650. Send a stamped, addressed envelope for a list of accredited courses.

Institute of Leisure & Amenity Management – Education &
Training Dept, ILAM House, Lower Basildon, Reading RG8
9NE. Tel: 01491 874222. Publishes *Careers in Leisure: A Brief
Guide* – distributed to careers centre and school careers libraries
(not available to individual enquirers).

Institute of Sport & Recreation Management – Giffard
House, 36–38 Sherrard St, Melton Mowbray, Leicestershire
LE13 1XJ. Tel: 01664 65531.

Sports Council – 16 Upper Woburn Place, London WC1H
0QP. Tel: 0171 273 1500.

Leisure Management, an AGCAS booklet for graduates, is avail-
able from CSU Despatch Dept, Armstrong House, Oxford
Road, Manchester M1 7ED. Tel: 0161 236 9816, ext 250/251.
Working in Leisure and *Working in Tourism*, both published by
COIC.

Community Practitioners and Health Visitors' Association
– 50 Southwark Street, London SE1 1UN. Tel: 0171 717 5000.

ENB Careers Section – PO Box 2EN, London W1A 2EN. Tel:
0171 391 6200/6205. Internet: http://www.enb.org.uk.
Produces information on all aspects of nursing, and lists of
courses in England.

Nursing and Midwifery Admissions Service (NMAS) –
Fulton House, Jessop Avenue, Cheltenham GL50 3SH. Handles
diploma-level nurse applications for England, and supplies
candidates with an application package. For a list of training
institutions in Wales, contact WNB, Floor 13, Pearl Assurance
House, Greyfriars Road, Cardiff CF1 3AG, then apply directly
to institutions.

**Welsh National Board for Nursing, Midwifery and Health
Visiting** – 13th Floor, Pearl Assurance House, Greyfriars Road,
Cardiff CF1 3AG. Provides information on training institutions
in Wales. Applications are made direct to individual training
schools.

Children's Nursing – a free booklet published by Health Service Careers, PO Box 204, London SE99 7UW.

Working in Nursing, published by COIC.

Careers in Nursing and Related Professions, published by Kogan Page.

Midwifery – Meet Someone New Every Day – a useful Health Service Careers publication available from PO Box 204, London SE99 7UW.

SPEECH THERAPY

Royal College of Speech & Language Therapists – 7 Bath Place, Rivington Street, London EC2A 3DR. Tel: 0171 613 3855. Send a stamped, addressed envelope for lists of undergraduate and postgraduate courses and careers information.

MEDICINE

British Medical Association – BMA House, Tavistock Square, London WC1H 9JP. Tel: 0171 387 4499. Publishes a booklet *Becoming a Doctor* which lists some other specialties and relevant addresses. Please send an A5 stamped, addressed envelope.

Royal College of Psychiatrists – 17 Belgrave Square, London SWIX 8PG. Tel: 0171 235 2351. Produces careers literature for intending psychiatrists.

Women in Medicine – 21 Wallingford Avenue, London W10 6QA. Tel: 0181 960 7446. Publishes *Careers for Women in Medicine – Planning and Pitfalls.*

Getting into Medicine, by Andrew Houghton and David Gray, published by Hodder & Stoughton.

Learning Medicine, by Peter Richards, published by the BMA.

Working in Medicine and Dentistry, published by COIC.